Effective Weight Loss

✔ TREATMENTS THAT WORK

Effective Weight Loss

An Acceptance-Based Behavioral Approach

WORKBOOK

EVAN M. FORMAN

MEGHAN L. BUTRYN

OXFORD
UNIVERSITY PRESS

OXFORD

UNIVERSITY PRESS

Oxford University Press is a department of the University of Oxford. It furthers
the University's objective of excellence in research, scholarship, and education
by publishing worldwide. Oxford is a registered trade mark of Oxford University
Press in the UK and certain other countries.

Published in the United States of America by Oxford University Press
198 Madison Avenue, New York, NY 10016, United States of America.

© Oxford University Press 2016

ISBN 978–0–19–023202–3

9 8 7 6 5 4 3 2 1

Printed by Sheridan Books, Inc., United States of America

One of the most difficult problems confronting patients with various disorders and diseases is finding the best help available. Everyone is aware of friends or family who have sought treatment from a seemingly reputable practitioner, only to find out later from another doctor that the original diagnosis was wrong or the treatments recommended were inappropriate or perhaps even harmful. Most patients, or family members, address this problem by reading everything they can about their symptoms, seeking out information on the Internet, or aggressively "asking around" to tap knowledge from friends and acquaintances. Governments and health-care policymakers are also aware that people in need do not always get the best treatments—something they refer to as *variability in health-care practices.*

Now health-care systems around the world are attempting to correct this variability by introducing *evidence-based practice.* This simply means that it is in everyone's interest that patients get the most up-to-date and effective care for a particular problem. Health-care policymakers have also recognized that it is very useful to give consumers of health care as much information as possible, so that they can make intelligent decisions in a collaborative effort to improve physical health and mental health. This series, Treatments *That Work*, is designed to accomplish just that. Only the latest and most effective interventions for particular problems are described in user-friendly language. To be included in this series, each treatment program must pass the highest standards of evidence available, as determined by a scientific advisory board. Thus when individuals suffering from these problems or their family members seek out an expert clinician who is familiar with these interventions and decides that they are appropriate, patients will have confidence they are receiving the best care available. Of course, only your health-care professional can decide on the right mix of treatments for you.

The program outlined in this workbook is the product of decades of research on the most effective weight loss treatments. Most traditional weight loss treatments are based on behavior modification, such as setting goals for calorie intake and exercise, identifying eating patterns, and changing problematic cues. While traditional behavior modification can be effective for weight loss, many individuals find that they don't lose as much weight as they would like, or they regain a substantial amount of weight following the initial loss. This workbook teaches a special kind of behavior modification, which is based on all of the critical components of standard programs, but adds to them novel strategies for making and maintaining changes in behavior that are critical to long-term weight loss.

The *Effective Weight Loss* program will help you identify and stay connected with meaningful reasons why weight loss is important to you and will help you make eating decisions more mindfully. You'll learn how to choose the healthiest behavior, even when it might not be the easiest or most pleasurable one. Committing to long-term changes in your lifestyle will help you maintain your weight loss and your health. This workbook is designed for use with your treatment provider, such as a psychologist, primary care physician, nutritionist, dietitian, or other professional helping you with weight loss. It provides session summaries, exercises, worksheets, handouts, and assignments to complete at home, while your provider follows the accompanying Clinician Guide to administer treatment over 25 sessions.

David H. Barlow, Editor-in-Chief
Treatments *ThatWork*
Boston, MA

References

Barlow, D. H. (2004). Psychological treatments. *American Psychologist, 59,* 869–878.

Barlow, D. H. (2010). Negative effects from psychological treatments: A perspective. *American Psychologist, 65*(2), 13–20.

Institute of Medicine. (2001). *Crossing the quality chasm: A new health system for the 21st century.* Washington, DC: National Academy Press.

McHugh, R. K., & Barlow, D. H. (2010). Dissemination and implementation of evidence-based psychological interventions: A review of current efforts. *American Psychologist, 65*(2), 73–84.

Accessing Treatments *ThatWork* Forms and Worksheets Online

All forms and worksheets from books in the TTW series are made available digitally shortly following print publication. You may download, print, save, and digitally complete them as PDFs. To access the forms and worksheets, please visit http://www.oup.com/us/ttw.

Contents

Acknowledgments *xiii*

Introduction: Information about Weight Loss and This Treatment Program *xv*

Chapter 1 Session 1: Welcome *1*

Chapter 2 Session 2: Calorie-Cutting Keys *11*

Chapter 3 Session 3: Goal Setting; Weighing and Measuring *25*

Chapter 4 Session 4: Labels, Planning, and Calorie Accounting *31*

Chapter 5 Session 5: Control What You Can, Accept What You Can't; The Home Food Environment *37*

Chapter 6 Session 6: Physical Activity and Willingness (Part 1) *43*

Chapter 7 Session 7: Willingness (Part 2) and Values *49*

Chapter 8 Session 8: Forming Good Habits and Flexibility *53*

Chapter 9 Session 9: Restaurant Eating; Handling Weekends and Special Occasions *59*

Chapter 10 Session 10: Barriers to Living a Valued Life *65*

Chapter 11 Session 11: Friends and Family *69*

Chapter 12   Session 12: Introduction to Defusion
and Urge Surfing   *75*

Chapter 13   Session 13: Strategies to Help Defuse
and Increase Willingness   *81*

Chapter 14   Session 14: Review of Dietary Principles, Mindless
Eating (Part 1), and Portion Sizes   *85*

Chapter 15   Session 15: Mindless Eating (Part 2) and Mindful
Decision-Making   *91*

Chapter 16   Session 16: Transitioning to Biweekly Meetings   *95*

Chapter 17   Session 17: Maintaining Losses Over
the Long Term   *101*

Chapter 18   Session 18: Willingness and Reducing Barriers
to Physical Activity   *107*

Chapter 19   Session 19: Committed Action   *111*

Chapter 20   Session 20: Overeating and Emotional Eating   *117*

Chapter 21   Session 21: Lapse Versus Relapse and Reversing Small
Weight Gains   *125*

Chapter 22   Session 22: Revisiting Commitment and Transition
to Monthly/Bimonthly Meetings   *135*

Chapter 23   Session 23: Maintaining Motivation   *139*

Chapter 24   Session 24: Looking Ahead   *145*

Chapter 25   Session 25: Celebrating Accomplishments   *155*

Appendix A   Keeping Track Form   *157*

Appendix B   In-Session Weight Change Record   *159*

Appendix C   Home Weight Change Record   *161*

Appendix D   Weekly Review   *163*

Appendix E   Worksheets   *165*

Acknowledgments

Behavioral weight loss treatment provides the foundation for the acceptance-based behavioral approach described in this book. Thus we are strongly indebted to the pioneering work of Drs. Thomas Wadden and Rena Wing (among others) who have been leaders in the field in developing, refining, and providing training in the behavioral weight loss principles that are embodied in this book. Additionally, the life-style modification materials used in the *Diabetes Prevention Program* and *Look AHEAD* clinical trials served as a starting point for developing the acceptance-based behavioral approach to weight loss. Those two land-mark clinical trials were funded by the National Institute of Diabetes and Digestive and Kidney Diseases (NIDDK). Material was also incorporated from the *Healthy Habits* treatment manual written by Dr. Hollie Raynor (which was created with support from NIDDK grant R01 DK074721).

This approach also is deeply rooted in the acceptance and commitment therapy literature. Drs. Steven Hayes, Kirk Strosahl, and Kelly Wilson have been pioneers in developing the theory and concepts that are apparent throughout this manual. Many exercises and metaphors have been adapted from the seminal book *Acceptance and Commitment Therapy* by Steven C. Hayes, Kirk D. Strosahl, and Kelly G. Wilson (New York: Guildford Press, 2011). Drs. G. Alan Marlatt, Marsha Linehan, and Debra Safer have developed innovative versions of behavioral therapy that also inspired much of the treatment material.

Drs. James Herbert and Michael Lowe both made important contributions to the development of this treatment approach. Several clinicians who were early providers of this treatment provided critical ideas for improvement, including Brooke Bailer, Vicki Clark, Kimberly Hoffman, Adrienne Juarascio, Danielle Kerns Clauss, and Alison Infield. Many other trainees were instrumental in providing feedback throughout the treatment development process and adapting the treatment manuals into book format, including Hallie Espel, Stephanie Goldstein, Stephanie Kerrigan, Lindsay Martin, Stephanie Manasse, Diane Rosenbaum, Katherine Schaumberg, and Leah Schumacher. Lauren Bradley deserves special thanks for the many important contributions she made to the original treatment manuals as well as her intelligent and careful proof-reading. Words cannot adequately express our gratitude to Britt Evans for coordinating this considerable undertaking. These books in large part owe their existence to her thoughtfulness, diligence, and grace. Special thanks go to Sarah Harrington and Kate Scheinman for serving as editor and development editor, respectively.

We are indebted to the NIDDK for funding three studies that supported the work of developing the original treatment manuals: *Mind Your Health* (R21 DK080430), *ENACT* (R01 DK092374) and *Mind Your Health II* (R01 DK095069). Finally, we thank the participants in those studies, from whom we learned so much about the challenges of weight control.

Introduction: Information about Weight Loss and This Treatment Program

Goals

- To understand the nature of weight control difficulties
- To decide if this program is a good fit for you
- To understand what program participation will involve

Understanding Weight Control Difficulties

You are not alone in seeking help to control your weight. The prevalence of obesity has increased dramatically in the past 50 years. In fact, two-thirds of adults in the United States (68%) are overweight or obese. In other words, it is now the *exception* to be lean! Scientists believe that adults have been gaining weight at these unprecedented levels largely because of changes in our lifestyles and powerful influences at the societal and environmental level. For example, many jobs require little physical activity, labor-saving devices in the home require less activity as we do chores, and more of us rely on cars, rather than walking, for transportation. Good-tasting food has become easily available, with a tremendous variety of manufactured options. Moreover, food now tends to be packaged and presented in much larger portion sizes in supermarkets, restaurants, and even cookbooks.

Humans are biologically driven to eat good-tasting food when it is available. For this reason, living in our current always-available food environment can feel like it requires near constant dietary restraint and willpower. In fact, scientists often refer to the modern Western environment as "obesogenic" because its characteristics push all of us who live in it to become obese. Research has made it clear that the high rates of obesity are *not* a result of individuals becoming "lazier" or less "able" to exert willpower. Instead, weight gain is understood to be a natural response to living in an unnatural environment.

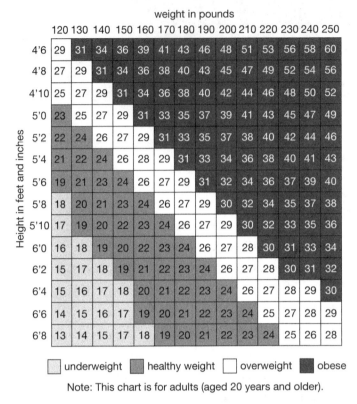

Figure 1

What Is Your Body Mass Index?

Should You Lose Weight?

Adults who are overweight or obese can benefit from weight loss treatment. To determine if you fall into this category, use Figure 1 to calculate your body mass index (BMI), which is a ratio of weight to height. Adults with a BMI higher than 25 kg/m² may benefit from weight loss.

Obesity can decrease your quality of life. It also can raise the risk of conditions such as diabetes, high blood pressure, and arthritis. Losing weight can improve quality of life and decrease risk for these negative health outcomes.

How Was This Program Developed?

This program is the outgrowth of decades of scientific research on weight loss treatment. Behavioral modification has been developed and improved over many years, and it is recommended as the first line of treatment for adults who wish to lose weight. A traditional approach to behavior modification focuses on setting specific goals for calorie intake and exercise, learning to identify patterns in eating and exercise behavior, and changing problematic cues for those behaviors. That approach has a tremendous body of evidence demonstrating that it can help the typical user lose 10% of body weight, which is superior to other available treatments such as taking a medication.

However, the traditional approach to behavior modification has two important limitations. First, although weight loss averages 10%, there are many individuals who do not respond sufficiently to that treatment and who do not meet weight loss goals. Second, most individuals regain a substantial amount of weight in the years following initial weight loss.

This workbook teaches a special form of behavior modification. It includes all of the critical skills that make the standard form of this approach effective, and it *also* teaches novel strategies that may make weight loss more effective for particular individuals. Research shows this program may be an especially good fit for you if you find yourself especially drawn to good-tasting foods, if you have trouble controlling your eating behavior, if you sometimes engage in emotional eating, or if you have a history of depression.

What Will the Program Involve?

This program is designed for use with a treatment provider. We recommend that you begin by having weekly visits with a specialist in behavior modification. You might work with a clinical psychologist, therapist, nutritionist, or other professional. If you are looking for a treatment provider, try a therapist directory in a reputable scientifically-based mental health organization, such as the Find-a-Therapist feature of the Association of Behavioral and Cognitive Therapies website (abct.org).

Your insurance provider can give you information about coverage for weight loss treatment and may be able to recommend providers to you as well.

In this program, you will learn several key skills:

■ You will learn how to monitor your eating behavior and consistently meet a calorie goal.

- You will gradually increase your physical activity and make exercise a habitual part of your lifestyle.
- You will anticipate and learn how to respond to particular challenges in your weight control, such as restaurant eating, holidays and special events, and life stressors.

These skills are a critical foundation for long-term weight loss. However, for some individuals, learning those skills is not sufficient, which is why this program also will offer you new ways of approaching your behavior change.

For instance, you will identify and stay connected with meaningful reasons why weight loss, healthy eating, and fitness are important *to you*. You will begin to make eating decisions more mindfully. The program will teach you how to choose the healthiest behavior, even when it is not the easiest or most pleasurable one. It will also help you commit to long-term changes in your lifestyle to maintain your weight loss and your health. This program is unique in combining traditional components of behavior modification, such as counting calories, with these newer approaches to behavior change.

This workbook is divided into 25 chapters. It is designed to be used in the order presented, because skills build upon each other. We recommend you follow one chapter per week for your first 12 to 16 weeks and then work with maintenance skills over a longer period of time. If you begin to regain weight, you may wish to revisit key skills and strategies from earlier sessions.

Special Considerations before Beginning This Treatment Program

This program is based on principles of behavior modification and on gold-standard behavioral treatments for weight loss. These treatments have demonstrated success and safety with overweight adults seeking to lose weight. However, certain medical factors suggest the need for a physician's approval and oversight and possibly the need to adjust certain aspects of the program. These factors include any medical condition (such as a heart condition) that could make it dangerous to engage in moderate or vigorous physical activity (exercise). If you cannot already walk two city blocks without stopping, you should consult a physician about how to safely increase your amount of physical activity over time. Similarly, if you have Type I (insulin-dependent) diabetes, you should consult your physician about whether to modify the program's dietary and physical activity guidelines, whether and how to adjust insulin dosages over time, and how to properly monitor your blood sugar levels. If you have a BMI above 50.0 kg/m², consult with your physician before starting this program to ensure that it is safe for you and for additional recommendations. Additionally, if you are pregnant or nursing, you should consult with your physician about individualized weight gain (or loss), diet, and exercise goals during pregnancy. While not specifically designed for pregnant or nursing women, virtually all weight control strategies and skills described in this program can be adapted for use during pregnancy and nursing when combined with individualized care from a health-care provider. Your doctor can help you determine appropriate weight gain or loss goals that will result in optimal health outcomes for both you and your child.

Generally speaking, if you experience psychological symptoms such as depression or anxiety, you can still complete this program. You may choose to see another clinician at the same time to focus on those symptoms. However, if you find that depression, anxiety, or other psychological symptoms are getting in the way of following the program, we recommend seeking treatment for those symptoms before pursuing weight loss.

Last, research shows that weight loss is more difficult for people who experience binge eating (eating very large amounts of food within a short time period and feeling out of control, i.e., not being able to stop even when they want to) or night eating (eating to fall asleep or waking up in the middle of the night to eat). Although you may still lose some weight with this program if you are experiencing these issues, we recommend seeking specialized treatment for binge eating or night eating before pursuing weight loss.

How Much Weight Can You Expect to Lose?

The very best weight loss programs result in an average weight loss of 10% after 12 months. Many people are disappointed by the idea of only losing 10% because their weight loss goals are far higher than 10%. However, remember that 10% represents an average weight loss; many people lose a higher percentage. Also, research shows that 10% weight loss is associated with numerous health benefits such as improvements in blood pressure, diabetes, cholesterol, and lowered risk for heart disease. Many people decrease the amount of medications they are taking or even come off medications completely with this amount of weight loss.

No matter your ultimate weight goal, we recommend starting the program with an initial weight loss goal of 10% of your body weight. Once a 10% loss is reached, you can set a new goal if desired.

Your biology and genetics, which are largely out of your control, may play a big role in how much weight you lose. However, one thing you can control is how closely you follow the program. *A critical scientific finding that has been demonstrated repeatedly is that the better people are at following program recommendations, the more weight they lose (and keep off).*

What Are Other Options for Weight Loss?

This program represents just one of many options for weight loss. We briefly discuss several alternatives in the following.

Standard Behavior Modification

Behavior modification has been widely studied in research. As we discussed at the beginning of this introduction, our program is based on behavioral modification and contains additional psychological strategies for maintaining behavior change in the long term. Our research suggests that certain people are more successful at standard behavioral modification than they are in our program. Specifically, if you are someone who is at the lower end of the spectrum when it comes to wanting to eat when in the presence of food cues (e.g., seeing or smelling food) even when not physically hungry or if you tend not to engage in emotional eating, you may want to consider standard behavior modification. You can work with your clinician to make a decision.

Medication

Several medications are approved and available for weight loss, including Orlistat, Meridia, and Phentermine. These medications do produce weight loss; however, they tend to result in less weight loss than participating in this program or standard behavior modification. Research indicates that medication might be a helpful addition to behavior modification programs. However, weight loss medications often come with serious side effects such as gastrointestinal problems, heart problems, and liver disease. As such, medication is generally only recommended if behavior modification fails and/or for those whose BMI is above 40 kg/m².

Bariatric Surgery

Surgical options for weight loss are typically for those who have a BMI of greater than 40.0 kg/m² or a BMI of greater than 35.0 kg/m² and medical comorbidities (e.g., Type II diabetes). Roux-en-Y gastric bypass and sleeve gastrectomy are the two safest and most effective procedures and typically result in 30% to 35% losses of body weight. Surgery poses risks of complications from nutritional deficiencies, undergoing anesthesia, wound infections, and developing blood clots.

Experiential Exercises, Metaphors, and Between-Session Assignments

You may have had the experience of having a lot of complicated information explained to you but had trouble understanding it in the first place or remembering it later on. In this workbook, we try to avoid this common problem by incorporating many exercises, discussions, and practices into the program. We believe that certain ideas cannot be fully appreciated simply by explanation. So some concepts are presented by way of metaphors that are designed to give you an alternative way to think about and absorb important concepts. For example, driving a bus in the direction you want to go, even though some annoying passengers are yelling at you to pull over, can be a metaphor for moving toward one's values (e.g., living a healthy lifestyle) even when doing so brings with it discomfort (like hunger or a loss of pleasurable eating). In addition, we believe that repeated practice is the best way to learn new skills. In our program, repeated practice of skills takes the form of between-session "Experiential Exercises" in which most weeks you will be assigned to deliberately practice a psychological skill and report back on your experience in the following session. These assignments will allow you to implement strategies you learn in session to the "real world." Your clinician will assign these Experiential Exercises in addition to weekly assignments such as self-monitoring of food intake, counting calories, and physical activity. This program requires a willingness to commit to your health!

Group Versus Individual Format

You will see that the material in this program is presented as if you are completing the program in a group. We developed and evaluated the program in a group format because it is more efficient to deliver material this way and because groups offer the advantages of greater accountability and support. However, we believe the program would be effective in individual format as well. You and your clinician can easily adapt the material to be delivered in an individual format if that is your preference or if a group program is not available.

Structure of Sessions

Sessions are typically structured in the following manner: (a) Check-In, (b) Skill Review, (c) new material (including behavioral and psychological strategies), and (d) Skill Builder assignments (to build specific skills). Weigh-ins occur before the start of the session. During check-in, you will report on your weight control behaviors for the week (e.g., calories consumed, minutes of physical activity). Your clinician will work with you to problem-solve any situations that came up since the last session, as well as any upcoming challenges to weight control. During the skill review, you and your clinician will discuss the Skill Builder assigned over the past week and discuss any successes or problems with implementing the strategies. New skills and concepts are then discussed. At the end of the session, the homework for the week (Skill Builders) is assigned.

Outline of the Program

Following this introduction there are 25 chapters, each of which supplements your work with your clinicians. You will see that for the first several weeks, the emphasis of the program is to get you started with the basics for weight loss such as self-monitoring your food intake/calories and weekly weighing. Beginning in Session 5, additional psychological strategies will be introduced and incorporated throughout the rest of the program. The 25 sessions are designed to be spread out over the course of a year, following a weekly schedule for 16 weeks, biweekly for six sessions, and monthly or bimonthly for the remainder of the sessions. This structure may be changed depending on your needs (e.g., earlier transition to biweekly or further continuation of weekly sessions), which you can discuss with your clinician.

Most people who complete this program will be actively trying to lose weight for the majority of the program. However, some people will hit their weight loss goal, plateau in their weight loss, or want to practice weight loss maintenance at different points of the program. We highly encourage you to regularly check in with your clinician about your weight loss versus weight maintenance goals. Weight loss maintenance is often more difficult than weight loss, so it may be important to practice maintenance during the program even if ultimately you'd like to lose more weight.

Control What You Can, Accept What You Can't

If you're like most people starting this program, you have tried to lose weight several times. You may have initially succeeded only to have regained your lost weight, or you may have not been able to lose much weight in the first place. Scientific studies point to two reasons that weight control is so difficult: our biology and our modern environment. First, as described earlier, human bodies are biologically hard-wired to desire high-calorie foods and to be at rest. Second, high-calorie foods are abundant and easily obtainable in our environment. Thus, our minds are filled with urges and thoughts about eating that run counter to our weight control goals.

Therefore, losing weight and keeping it off are enormously challenging. This program aims to meet this challenge by teaching you a comprehensive set of strategies. We present these strategies, in part, through the framework of *control what you can, accept what you can't*. This framework divides life into that over which we have direct control (essentially behaviors we can choose to perform, including those that would modify our immediate surroundings) and that which we don't (the internal workings of our bodies, including our thoughts, feelings, and sensations, and the wider environment). *Control what you can* refers to weight control behaviors that are changeable and controllable such as the way you walk to work, what you put into a shopping cart, leaving your house keys in a gym locker on the way to work, putting extra portions in a freezer before sitting down for a meal, taking another step on a walk, and making a lunch to bring to work. *Accept what you can't* refers to accepting a less comfortable psychological or physical state—for example, tiredness, anxiety, low motivation, hunger, cravings, urges to eat a particular food or type of food (like a sweet after dinner), imagining how good a food will taste, thoughts about giving up and being a failure, and thoughts that rationalize breaking your diet or physical activity plan. *Accept what you can't* also includes being willing to choose behaviors that are consistent with your values even if that is the less pleasurable option, clarifying values by which you would like to live your life, and learning to keep such values in the front and center of your mind so as not to slip into mindless behavior that is biased toward choosing unhealthy foods and staying at rest.

Overall, our program fully integrates the key strategies needed for long-term weight control (*Control what you can*). However, it also provides strategies for navigating the natural barriers for enacting such behaviors in the long term, such as the wider food environment and our biologically driven desire for unhealthy foods, which manifests itself in thoughts, feelings, and sensations (*Accept what you can't*). We describe this framework in more detail in Session 5.

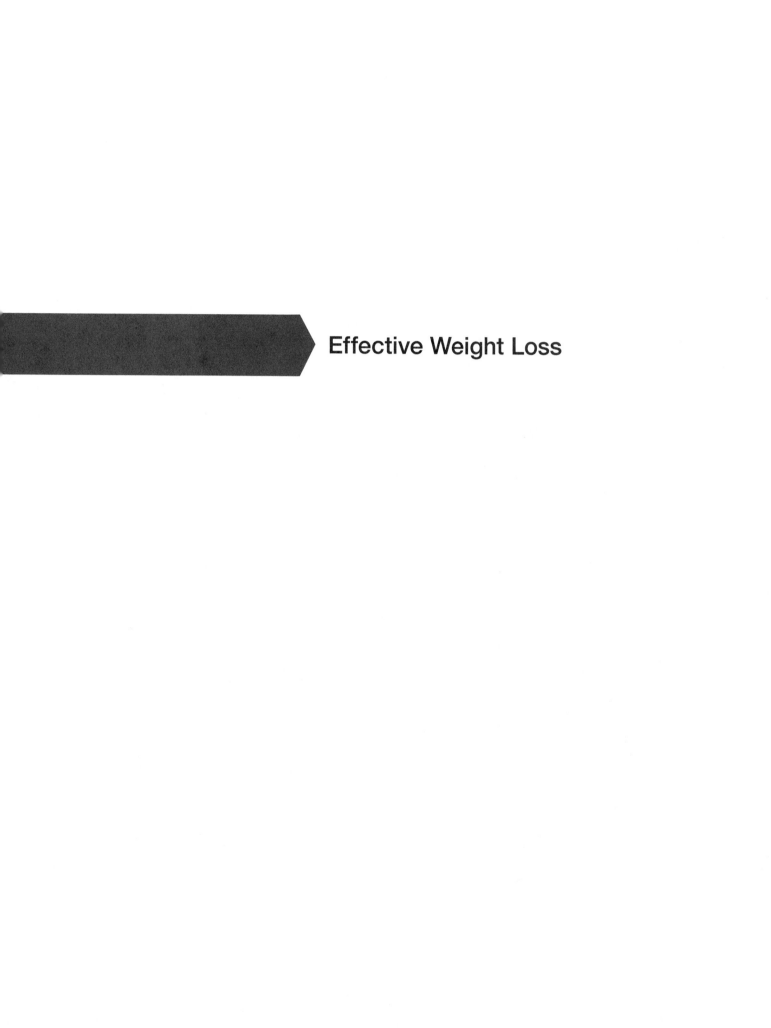

Effective Weight Loss

Goals for This Session

- To provide an overview of the treatment used in this program
- To introduce group policies and procedures
- To develop weight, calorie, and activity goals
- To start monitoring calories
- To start cutting back on high-calorie foods
- To discuss assignments for the coming week

Treatment Overview

The philosophy of the program is based on several assumptions regarding weight, health, and weight loss.

1. For people who are overweight, weight loss improves health and well-being. Weight loss is associated with improvements in blood pressure, cholesterol, sleep apnea, arthritis, blood sugar, mood, and body image. These improvements can be achieved with modest weight losses of about 10% of your current body weight. For someone who currently weighs 200 pounds, this would be a weight loss of about 20 pounds.

2. Long-term change in behaviors is necessary to successfully lose weight and to maintain weight loss (to keep lost weight off). The program is different from many others because it is specially designed to help you maintain weight loss in the long term. The program will provide

extensive instruction in the long-term modification of eating and exercise habits. You may have had the experience of losing weight and later regaining it; we hope that the skills you learn in this program will allow you to keep off the weight you lose, even after your sessions end.

3. Overwhelming scientific evidence shows that reduced calorie intake is the most important determinant of weight loss. So, our approach focuses on setting and keeping to a calorie goal. It allows for eating a wide variety of foods and portion control of high-calorie foods (i.e., not limiting your eating to a particular type of food or completely cutting out a type of food, such as carbohydrates). Increased energy expenditure is the second most important way to succeed, so this program also focuses on setting and keeping exercise goals.

4. Specific psychological skills and abilities help with weight control:

   (a) Long-term weight loss is difficult, in part because we are biologically engineered to eat delicious food, and in the modern world, great-tasting food is always available. This availability generates a nearly constant desire to eat and sometimes cravings to eat particular high-calorie foods. Similarly, the modern world encourages us to be sedentary rather than active.

   (b) You have probably tried to address these challenges by doing things like trying to convince yourself to eat a certain way or to exercise, exerting more willpower, or pushing away your hunger/cravings. Often these approaches do not work well, especially in the long term.

   (c) This program is unique in that it will give you some new tools for responding to challenges of long-term behavior change. We will teach you skills that we have found enable you to choose what to eat and how active to be, even despite challenging conditions. We start introducing these skills in Session 5.

Guidelines for Success

Whether you are receiving group or individual treatment, there are a number of behaviors that will help you be more successful.

1. Do your very best to *come to every scheduled meeting*! This is important even when you're having a hard time.
2. Be on time. Call if you can't come.

3. Complete Skill Builders each week.
4. Complete Keeping Track Forms every day.
5. Bring your workbook and weekly records to every meeting.

Group Participation

A group is like a team, and, if you are receiving group treatment, we have several additional recommendations for getting the most out of your team. By working together, group members can support and encourage each other, share ideas to solve problems, and motivate one another. Being a good group member is a responsibility to others. It is also the best way to help yourself to succeed. In addition to the guidelines mentioned previously, some guidelines for group participation are:

1. Take part in sharing your ideas with other group members.
2. Let everyone have a chance to share. Be careful how much time you spend talking.
3. Be willing to really listen to other people's concerns. Do what you can to show you understand and care. Share what has worked for you.
4. Do not repeat to other people outside of the group anything personal that's talked about in the group.
5. Be attentive.
6. Respect other people's ideas. Avoid putting others down.
7. Eat outside of the group, either before or after the session.
8. Turn off your cell phone before group begins.

Keeping Track of Your Weight

Your clinician will keep track of your weight by weighing you (in private) before every session. It is a good habit for you to weigh yourself regularly at home, as well. During the initial phase of weight loss, we recommend that you weigh yourself once a week at home. Later, when you have moved into a "weight maintenance" phase (when your goal is to maintain your current weight, rather than to lose weight), we recommend that you weigh yourself daily at home. In order for weighing to be most useful, you should weigh yourself under consistent conditions. In particular, weigh yourself:

- When you first get up in the morning
- After using the bathroom
- Before eating or drinking

It is very important to record your weight each time you weigh yourself. By keeping and reviewing a record over time, you (and your clinician) will be able to notice trends and make adjustments. We recommend recording your weight visually, using a weight graph. You can use a website or smartphone app to do this, or you can use the Home Weight Change Record shown in Appendix C of this workbook. The Home Weight Change Record includes both a graph and a table version. Choose whichever format you prefer to track your weight at home. You may find that your scale at home differs from your clinician's scale by 1 to 2 pounds; thus, a separate In-Session Weight Change Record (Appendix B) is provided to track your weights that are measured at each session. During the first phase of the program, when you are attending sessions on a weekly basis, the In-Session Weight Change Record may be most useful to you. However, once sessions become less frequent and you are in a maintenance phase, regularly completing and monitoring the Home Weight Change Record becomes essential.

Developing Weight, Calorie, and Activity Goals

During this program, you will set weekly and monthly weight-loss goals. The program is designed to achieve a 1–2 pound weight loss per week. This rate of weight loss was chosen because it has proven to be the most successful and the safest. Attempting to lose weight much faster is unlikely to be sustainable in the long run. Moreover, very rapid decreases in weight can cause medical problems, such as gallstones. By five months, most people will achieve a 10% weight loss or more.

Part of the first few weeks of treatment involves finding a calorie goal that results in healthy weight loss for you. To start off, you will choose your own calorie goal within a range.

In order to achieve a weight loss of 1 to 2 pounds a week, we recommend picking an initial calorie goal in the range shown in Table 1-1.

Table 1-1 Initial Calorie Goals

Your Starting Weight	Calorie Goal
<250 pounds	1,200–1,500
>250 pounds	1,500–1,800

After today's session, identify a specific number within your range as a tester calorie target. For example, if you weigh 225 pounds, you might choose 1,300 calories as your initial calorie target. Set a specific calorie target right now, using Table 1-1 as your guide.

My initial calorie target: _____

This program also has set exercise goals.

For the coming week, set a goal of 15 minutes of brisk walking (or another aerobic activity), three days per week, for a minimum of 45 minutes per week.

The physical activity goals will gradually increase, up to 250 minutes per week, as shown in Table 1-2.

Table 1-2 Physical Activity Goals by Program Week

Session	Days per Week	Minutes per Day	Total for Week
1–5	3	15	45
6–7	3	20	60
8–9	4	20	80
10–11	4	25	100
12–15	4	30	120
16–17	5	30	150
18–19	5	40	200
20	5	45	225
21 and up	5	50	250

Getting Started: Self-Monitoring

To help you lose weight, our goal is to help you to monitor your food intake and, more specifically, monitor your *calorie* intake. Eating *too many* calories from any type of food makes us gain weight, so it is particularly important to monitor your calorie intake. In the next session we will provide more information about how to track your calorie intake, but before you start trying to change your eating habits, you should learn about your current food and beverage consumption. Once you know more about your current eating habits—especially the amount of calories you take in—you will be ready to begin to make modifications. Changing and maintain your eating can be a difficult challenge. The *most important* way to accomplish successful dietary change is to note everything you eat and drink every day. You should:

- Be thorough (write down *everything* you eat/drink, except for water)
- Be accurate (read labels)
- Be complete (include *all information*—time, amount, type, and description of food)

One day of self-monitoring (without calorie intake) is shown in Figure 1-1. See Appendix A for a blank copy of this food record form, which we call your Keeping Track Form. You will want to make multiple copies of this form so that you can complete a new one every day. Alternatively, there are several other options for tracking what you eat and drink, including online forms (try searching for terms like "printable food diary"), websites (e.g., MyFitnessPal), and smartphone apps (e.g., MyFitnessPal, MyNetDiary, SparkPeople).

Cutting Back on High-Calorie Foods and Drinks

As previously noted, eating *too many* calories from any type of food will lead to weight gain. However, foods with *fat, oils, and sugar* are especially dense in calories. Yet these foods, especially sugary foods, are not particularly filling. As a result, we tend to eat more of these foods to feel satisfied. Therefore, reducing your intake of high-fat and high-sugar foods can be a good way to start reducing your overall caloric intake.

As a first step in reducing your total energy intake, cut back on the foods in the Cutting Back on High Calorie Foods Form (Worksheet 1-1). Cutting back means eating one-third less than you normally do. Examples would be drinking two cans of soda per day instead of three, using two-thirds of a tablespoon of salad dressing instead of 1 tablespoon, and eating cereal with 8 g of sugar instead of one with 12 g of sugar. Of course if you can reduce these foods by a further amount or eliminate altogether, that is even better.

The more specifically you plan, the more likely you will meet your goals. So, next you should plan specifically which food/drinks you would like to cut back on this upcoming week. In order to do this, complete Worksheet 1-1 in Appendix E.

Day of the week: Monday		Date: 2/20/15	
Time	**Food (Amount and Description)**	**Calories**	
8:00	1 c Cheerios		
	3/4 c skim milk		
	1 c coffee with 2 tbsp creamer		
10:00	Medium banana		
12:00p	6" white hoagie roll		
	4 oz deli Turkey		
	2 oz iceberg lettuce		
	2 slices tomato		
	1 oz bag potato chips		
3:00p	1 yogurt		
	Medium apple		
6:30p	4 oz grilled chicken breast		
	1/2 c brown rice with 1 tsp butter		
	3/4 c steamed broccoli		
	White dinner roll		
8:00p	1/2 c mint choc chip ice cream		

Figure 1-1

Example of a Completed Keeping Track Form

Each session will end with a Skill Builder assignment for you to complete prior to the next session. The purpose of these Skill Builders is to practice the skills that are discussed during session.

Complete the following assignments before the next meeting:

☐ *Activity*: Exercise (e.g., brisk walking) for 15 minutes × 3 days.

☐ *Behavior*: Record all foods and drinks using the Keeping Track Form in Appendix A (time, amount, type and description of food) consumed except water. (Make sure to have made multiple copies of the Keeping Track Form so that you can start a new one each day.) Use a calorie-tracking book or website, measuring cups, food scale, and nutrition labels to determine caloric intake (to the best of your ability).

☐ *Calories*: Based on the Cutting Back on High Calorie Foods Form (Worksheet 1-1), reduce intake of high-calorie foods by one-third. In your Keeping Track Form, mark times when you were successful (checkmark or "yes"), were unsuccessful (X or "no"), or weren't sure whether or not you were successful ("?") in cutting back on the high-calorie foods and drinks you were attempting to cut back on. See Figure 1-1 in the workbook for an example of a completed form, and Figure 1-2 for an example of how to begin reducing intake of high-calorie foods.

Try to stay within your target calorie range (1,200–1,500 for <250 lbs.; 1,500–1,800 for >250 lbs.).

☐ *Days Recorded*: Record every day.

☐ *Experiential Exercise*: N/A

☐ *Reminder*: Complete your Check-In sheet before the next session. Also, don't forget to bring your Keeping Track Forms (or printout that includes foods, time eaten, and calories).

To help you become more aware of changes you may want to make in your diet, as well as to help you track your progress with your goal of avoiding or cutting back on (by at least one-third) high-calorie foods and drinks this week, mark the following in your Keeping Track Form:

☐ Mark with "Yes" (or a checkmark) meals/snacks where you were able to successfully met your goal of avoiding/cutting back (by at least one-third) your intake of a high-calorie food/drink.

☐ Mark with "No" (or an "X") meals/snacks where you were not able to successfully meet your goal of avoiding/cutting back on (by at least one-third) high-calorie foods and drinks.

☐ Mark with a "?" meals/snacks where you had difficulty knowing whether or not you met your goal of avoiding/cutting back on (by at least one-third) high-calorie foods and drinks.

☐ Examples of success: not having a food/drink at a meal or snack (or between meals/snacks) that you normally would; having at least one-third less than you normally would

☐ Examples of unsuccessful attempts: having a normal amount (or more than normal) of a high-calorie food when you had planned to have one-third less of that food/drink this week

Day _____ Date 2/20/15

Time	Description	Calories		"Yes" (normally have whole milk)
8:00	Bowl ...rios			
	Skim milk			
	Coffee with creamer			"Yes" (normally have a donuts)
10:00	Banana			
12:00p	Hoagie			"No" (had normal amount of chips, not one-third less as planned)
	Deli Turkey			
	Lettuce			
	Tomato			
	1oz. bag potato chips			
3:00p	1 yogurt			
	Medium apple			

Time	Food (Amount and Description)	Calories
6:30p	Chicken breast	
	Rice with butter	
	Broccoli	
	Roll	
8:00p	Mint choc chip ice cream	

"?" (had a little less ice cream than I intended, but not sure if it was one-third less)

"Yes" (normally have a few cookies at 10 pm)

Daily Totals   ____ ____

Type of Physical Activity	Minutes
Total minutes daily physical activity	

Total Steps   ____

Figure 1-2

Tracking Progress With Cutting Back

Instructions: Complete the following items *before* you attend Session 2.

A. *Activity*: Last week I exercised on _____ days, for an average of _____ minutes per day.

(The goal for last week was 3 × 15 minutes of activity.)

B. *Behavior*: I did/did not *(circle one)* attempt to use a calorie-tracking book or website, measuring cups, food scale, and nutrition labels to determine my caloric intake (to the best of my ability).

C. *Calories*: I did/did not *(circle one)* cut back on my intake of high-fat and high-sugar foods by at least one-third.

I did/did not *(circle one)* mark in my Keeping Track Form times when I was successful (checkmark or "yes"), was unsuccessful ("X" or "no"), or wasn't sure whether I was successful ("?") in cutting back on these foods/drinks.

I did/did not *(circle one)* stay within my target calorie range.

D. *Days Recorded*: I recorded my intake for _____ of the past seven days.

E. *Experiential Exercise*: N/A

CHAPTER 2 — Session 2: Calorie-Cutting Keys

Goals for This Session

- To review events of the past week and check in about progress
- To review the importance of self-monitoring
- To start reducing caloric intake
- To discuss assignments for the coming week

Self-Monitoring

Self-monitoring is a critical part of this program. The benefits include:

- Identifying the patterns in what, when, where, and why you eat.
- Learning how to correctly estimate how much you are eating. As a result, you will be less likely to underestimate how much you have eaten.
- Understanding why you may have dietary lapses.

Completing food records (the Keeping Track Form in Appendix A) will be one way that you self-monitor.

Each day, record the following information in your Keeping Track Form:

- Time of meal or snack
- Food type, description, and method of preparation
- Amount (it is critical to weigh and measure your food)

Complete the form throughout the day immediately after eating. The longer you wait to record, the less accurate your recall will be.

Calorie Tracking

Today you will be completing the Calorie Tracking Example Worksheet (Worksheet 2-1) in Appendix E. Once you complete Worksheet 2-1, use the answers in Figure 2-5 at the end of this chapter to check your calorie accuracy.

Beginning to Reduce Caloric Intake

Through experimentation over the next few weeks, this program will help you establish an ideal calorie goal, which will lead to weight loss of 1 to 2 pounds per week.

Energy Balance

Calorie balance is the balance between the calories (energy) you (a) take in by eating and (b) use up by being active and keeping your body running.

When you eat food, you take in calories. Calories in food come from fat, carbohydrates (starches and sugars), protein, or alcohol. Fat is the highest in calories per gram.

Calories also measure the energy you use up. Your body uses up energy through the activities it performs automatically to stay alive (like breathing, circulating blood, thinking, and digesting food) and when you are active (like when you're exercising).

Your weight is the result of the balance between food (calories in) and activity (calories out). See Figure 2-1 for an illustration. In order to lose weight, you must eat fewer calories than your burn through metabolism and exercise. This program will help you to reduce your calorie intake and increase your physical activity.

You should aim to lose 1 to 2 pounds per week. To lose this amount, you will need to eat and drink approximately 500 fewer calories a day than you are now. For example, if your current diet consists of 2,000 calories per day, you will now need to consume 1,500 calories per day to lose

Figure 2-1

Calorie Balance

weight. Trial and error will determine which calorie intake goal produces 1 to 2 pounds of weight loss for you each week.

We recommend an initial weight loss goal of 7–10% of body weight. After you have reached your weight loss goal, you will learn how to maintain reductions in your calorie intake so that over time the energy you take in equals the energy that you burn, and your weight stays steady. This program will help you learn how to adopt dietary changes that can be maintained over the long term. Slowly returning to old eating habits can be tempting after initial weight loss success, but that is likely to cause weight gain; you will learn how to respond to that temptation and stay committed to your new, healthier lifestyle.

TOP: Tips for Starting Out

These three TOP tips can be useful for starting to reduce calories:

- *Time your eating:* Eat on a regular schedule and avoid going more than 4 to 6 hours without eating. When you get intensely hungry, it can be harder to make healthy food choices.
- *Optimize your environment:* Stock up on healthy, low-calorie foods (such as vegetables, fruits, whole grains, lean sources of protein, and low-fat dairy products). When these healthy foods are visible and easily available, eating them becomes more likely. Also, consider the types and quantities of high-calorie foods (such as chips, cookies, and whole milk) at your house and/or workplace. Remove the foods that are most tempting to you.
- *Plan ahead:* Planning is a critical skill for long-term weight control. From shopping to exercise to high-risk situations, making a plan really helps. Anticipate what challenges may arise, so you can create

a plan of attack ahead of time. Get in the habit of making a meal plan on a weekly or daily basis. Ideally, when you get up each morning you will have a plan for what, when, and where you will eat all of your meals and snacks that day.

Ways to Reduce Calorie Intake and Increase Healthy Eating

- Increase intake of *fruits and vegetables*: Stay full by adding these to dishes, use fruit and vegetables for snacks, and use fruit for satisfying a sweet craving.
- Eat lean sources of *protein*: Avoid meats, fish, and poultry that is cooked with butter or oil. Instead, eat meat that is baked, broiled, or grilled. Remove skin and visible fat.
- Eat *whole grains* when consuming carbohydrates: These are not necessarily lower in calories than refined versions, but they are more filling. Note that packaging (e.g., for bread) can be misleading when it comes to whole grains.
- *Limit calories from beverages*: Beverages are not as filling as solid food. Also, limit alcohol intake, because alcohol is empty calories that also can trigger additional eating (and less physical activity).
- Use *sample meal plans*: See meal plans in Figures 2-2, 2-3, and 2-4, as a resource for planning meals and snacks.
- Pay attention to *what foods are available in your home*: Set yourself up for success by reducing availability of tempting, high-calorie foods and make healthy choices available.

Strive for a Better Diet

Fruits and Vegetables

The following are some commonly available fruits and vegetables. Check off at least three fruits and three vegetables that you will eat in the next week. Make a note of how you will eat them. For example, you might mix tomato and spinach with scrambled eggs, eat baby carrots for an afternoon snack, or use frozen strawberries in a smoothie.

Vegetables

☐ Asparagus _____
☐ Beets _____
☐ Broccoli _____
☐ Brussels sprouts _____

- ☐ Cabbage _____
- ☐ Carrots _____
- ☐ Cauliflower _____
- ☐ Celery _____
- ☐ Collard greens _____
- ☐ Cucumber _____
- ☐ Eggplant _____
- ☐ Green beans _____
- ☐ Kale _____
- ☐ Lettuce _____
- ☐ Mushrooms _____
- ☐ Peppers _____
- ☐ Squash _____
- ☐ Tomato _____
- ☐ Zucchini _____
- ☐ Other vegetables _____

Fruits

- ☐ Apples _____
- ☐ Bananas _____
- ☐ Blueberries _____
- ☐ Cantaloupe _____
- ☐ Cherries _____
- ☐ Grapes _____
- ☐ Grapefruit _____
- ☐ Pears _____
- ☐ Honeydew _____
- ☐ Oranges _____
- ☐ Peaches _____
- ☐ Strawberries _____
- ☐ Watermelon _____
- ☐ Other fruits _____

Protein

Getting enough protein is important for staying full. Circle the following items that you will use for meals and snacks as sources of protein this week:

Eggs	Nuts	Fish	Turkey
Yogurt	Beans	Beef	Pork
Cheese	Tofu	Chicken	

- Watching portion size is important with foods such as nuts and cheese, because these high-protein foods are high in fat.
- When preparing foods such as fish or chicken, it is important to use low-calorie methods of cooking. Do not bread these foods, fry them, or sauté them with high amounts of oil or butter. Roast, bake, grill, broil, steam, or sauté with a nonstick spray.
- Remove the skin from foods such as turkey and chicken.
- Remove visible fat from foods such as steak and pork.
- Choose lean cuts of beef, turkey, and pork.
- Rather than using butter, oil, cheese, or cream to add flavor when cooking, add lower calorie choices such as the following:

Hot sauce	Lemon or lime juice	Herbs
Mustard	Soy sauce	Spices

Grains, Pasta, Bread, and Cereal

Whole grains do not necessarily have fewer calories than refined carbohydrates, but they will keep you full longer. Breads, cold cereals, hot cereals, pasta, and rice are examples of foods that may (or may not!) be made with whole grains.

You can tell if a food is whole grain by looking at the package and label. Look for the words "whole grain." Check the ingredient list too. The first ingredient listed is present in the highest quantity by weight. If the food is high in whole grain, it will be listed first.

You may think that some ingredients are whole grain when in reality they are not. For instance, some items labeled multigrain, 100% wheat, stone ground, or pumpernickel may not be whole grain. Also look at the amount of fiber in one serving. Most whole-grain products will have 2 to 3 grams of fiber per serving whereas refined grain products will have 1 gram. Table 2-1 shows an example of how to choose a wholewheat bread.

Table 2-1 Example of Whole-Grain Ingredients

		Ingredients of two different breads
1. Find the ingredient list on the bread wrapper	This one *is* whole wheat	Example 1: *Whole-wheat flour*, water, wheat gluten, corn syrup, honey, soybean oil, yeast
2. Choose bread that lists whole wheat as the first ingredient	This one is *not* whole wheat	Example 2: *Wheat flour*, water, whole-wheat flour, corn syrup, honey, soybean oil, yeast

Even though Example 2 in Table 2-1 contains wholewheat flour, it is not considered a whole-grain product because whole-wheat flour is not the first ingredient listed.

When choosing bread products, consider the following:

- On labels, "wheat flour" is another name for "white flour."
- "Enriched" means that iron and B vitamins have been added, but most of the fiber, zinc, and other vitamins and minerals are absent.
- "Whole wheat" means all parts of the wheat kernel are included.
- Whole grains do not necessarily have fewer calories than refined carbohydrates, but they will keep you full longer.
- Bread wrappers can be misleading—look at the ingredient list instead.
- Look for grams of fiber per serving on the Nutrition Facts label.

Beverages

Reducing calories from beverages is important because drinks tend not to be very filling and can be high in sugar.

- If you drink juice, start having a piece of fruit in its place.
- If you drink coffee or tea, gradually cut down on sugar and cream. You can gradually decrease your sugar/cream amount week by week, until you fully switch to artificial sweeteners and nonfat milk, or having your drink black with no sweetener. With time your taste buds will adapt.
- If you drink soda, switch to diet soda or unsweetened or low-calorie carbonated water/seltzer.

Each breakfast menu below contains approximately 200-300 calories. Make your food choices from the lists that follow. Foods marked with an asterisk (*) are good sources of fiber.

Menu 1: Cereal

Cold or hot cereal (1 serving)
Milk (4 ounces)
Fruit (1 serving)

Menu 2: Toast and fruit

Bread (1 serving)
Jam, jelly, fat-free cream cheese, or low-calorie margarine (1 serving)
Fruit (2 servings)

Menu 3: Egg (fresh cooked or hard boiled) and fruit

Egg (2 servings)
Fruit (1 serving)

Menu 4: Yogurt and fruit

Low-fat yogurt (1 serving)
Fruit (2 servings)

Menu 5: Egg and veggie scramble

Egg (2 servings)
Vegetable (2 servings)

Menu 6: Granola, yogurt, and fruit parfait

Low-fat yogurt (1 serving)
Granola (1 serving)
Fruit (1 serving)

Food	Amount	Calories	Fat (g)
Cereal			
* Bran Flakes	3/4 cup	100	0
* Cheerios (plain)	1 cup	110	0
* Oatmeal, cooked, no fat added, unsweetened	1/2 cup cooked or 1 pkg instant (plain)	100	2
* Shredded Wheat, Spoon Size	1/2 cup	85	1
* Kashi Go Lean	3/4 cup	105	1
Milk, Yogurt			
Skim milk	4 oz.	43	0
1% milk	4 oz.	51	2
Low-fat yogurt	6-8 oz.	100–120	0
Bread			
* Whole wheat toast	1 slice	100	1
Egg			
One egg (x-large)	1	85	6

Food	Amount	Calories	Fat (g)
Vegetables			
Mixed, cooked (spinach, tomatoes, peppers, etc.)	1/2 cup	25	0
Granola			
Granola	1/4 cup	150	8
Fruit			
* Banana, 8" long	1/2	48	0
* Orange, 2 5/8" diam.	1	62	0
* Grapefruit, 4" diam.	1/2	47	0
* Strawberries, fresh	1 cup	46	0
* Grapes, all kinds	1/2 cup	57	0
* Pear, 2 ½" diam.	1	98	1
Jam, jelly, fat-free cream cheese, reduced-fat margarine			
Jam or jelly, regular (any flavor)	2 tsp	32	0
Cream cheese, fat-free	2 Tbsp	30	0
Margarine, low-cal	2 tsp	34	4

Figure 2-2

Meal Plan: Breakfast Menus

Each lunch menu below contains approximately 300-400 calories. Make your food choices from the lists that follow. Foods marked with an asterisk (*) are good sources of fiber.

Menu 1

Salad greens (2 servings)
Salad dressing (1 serving)
Chicken, turkey, salmon, tuna, or ham (2 servings)
Fruit (1 serving)

Menu 2

Chicken, turkey, salmon, tuna, or ham (2 servings)
Condiment (1 serving)
Bread (1 serving)
Fruit (1 serving)

Menu 3

Salad
Salad dressing, low-calorie or fat-free
  (1 serving)
Beans, cottage cheese, tofu, or hummus
  (2 servings)

Menu 4

Salad
Salad dressing, low-calorie or fat-free
  (1 serving)
Low-calorie frozen entree

Food	Amount	Calories	Fat (g)
Chicken, turkey, salmon, tuna, or ham			
Tuna, canned in water, drained	3 oz	99	1
Salmon, canned in water, drained	3 oz	118	5
Turkey breast, processed luncheon meat, oven-roasted	3 oz	90	5
Chicken breast, processed luncheon meat, oven-roasted	3 oz	90	3
Ham, processed luncheon meat, sliced or chopped	3 oz	90	3
Vegetarian proteins			
Cottage cheese, 1% milk fat	1/2 cup	82	1
* Hummus (chickpea dip), plain	2 Tbsp	79	4
Tofu, regular, no fat added	1/2 cup	94	6
* Beans & peas, dried, no fat added	1/2 cup ckd	129	1
* Chickpeas (garbanzo beans)	1/2 cup ckd	134	2
Bread			
Pita or pocket bread, 7" diam.	1/2 pita	96	1
* Whole wheat bread	1 slice	100	1
* Brown rice	1/2 cup ckd	105	1

Food	Amount	Calories	Fat (g)
Salad			
Lettuce with sliced tomatoes and carrots	1 cup	15	0
Frozen entrees or dinners, low calorie			
Any with ≤ 350 calories and ≤ 10 grams of fat			
Fruit			
* Apple, 2 ¾" diam.	1 each	81	0
* Orange, fresh, 2 ⅝" diam.	1 each	62	0
* Peach, fresh, 2 ½" diam. or canned in water	1 each	37	1
* Pear, fresh, 2 ½" diam. or canned in water	1 each	98	1
* Pineapple, fresh or canned in juice	1/2 cup	38	0
* Banana, 8" long	1/2	48	0
Condiments, salad dressing			
Mayonnaise, low-calorie	1 Tbsp	49	5
Olive oil and vinegar	1 Tbsp	70	12
Salad dressing, low calorie	1 Tbsp	43	1–3
Mustard	2 Tbsp	24	1

Figure 2-3

Meal Plan: Lunch Menus

Each dinner menu below contains approximately 500-600 calories. Make your food choices from the lists that follow. Foods marked with an asterisk (*) are good sources of fiber.

Menu 1

- ☐ Salad greens (2 servings)
- ☐ Salad dressing (1 serving)
- ☐ Fish or poultry, cooked without fat, skin removed (1 serving)
- ☐ Pasta, potato, or rice (1 serving)
- ☐ Vegetable (1 serving)

Menu 2

- ☐ Beans, cottage cheese, tofu, or hummus (1 serving)
- ☐ Rice (2 servings) or 1 serving of pasta or potato

Food	Amount	Calories	Fat (g)
Fish or poultry, cooked without fat			
Fish, fresh or frozen, no fat or breading	3 oz	90	1
Turkey, ground, lean (breast only)	3 oz	160	8
Turkey, light meat, skin removed	3 oz	140	3
Chicken, white meat, skin removed	3 oz	141	3
Vegetarian proteins			
Cottage cheese, 1% milk fat	1/2 cup	82	1
* Hummus (chickpea dip), plain	2 Tbsp	79	4
Tofu, regular, no fat added	1/2 cup	94	6
* Beans & peas, dried, no fat added	1/2 cup ckd	129	1
* Chickpeas (garbanzo beans)	1/2 cup ckd	134	2
Pasta, potato, or rice			
Pasta, white or * whole wheat, plain	1 cup ckd	197	1
Rice, white, * wild, or * brown	1/2 cup ckd	105	1
Potato, mashed, made with skim milk, and no fat added	1 cup	156	0
Potato, boiled without skin	Medium	200	0
* Sweet potato or yam, baked in skin	1/2 cup	131	0
Margarine or salad dressing, low-calorie, reduced-fat, or fat-free			
Olive oil and vinegar	1 Tbsp	70	12
Salad dressing, low-calorie	1 Tbsp	43	1-3
Margarine, low-calorie	1 tsp	34	4

Food	Amount	Calories	Fat (g)
Vegetables			
* Broccoli, cooked	1 cup ckd	52	0
* Brussels sprouts, cooked	1 cup ckd	66	0
* Cabbage, red or green, cooked	1 cup ckd	32	0
* Carrots, cooked	1 cup ckd	70	0
* Cauliflower, cooked	1 cup ckd	34	0
* Corn, whole kernel, cooked	1/2 cup ckd	66	0
* Green beans, cooked	1 cup ckd	38	0
* Peas, green, cooked	1/2 cup ckd	62	0
* Peas, snow, cooked	1 cup ckd	50	0
* Peppers, bell, cooked	1 cup ckd (chopped)	38	0
* Spinach, cooked	1/2 cup ckd	54	0
* Squash, summer, cooked	1/2 cup ckd	44	0
* Squash, acorn, butternut, or hubbard	1 cup ckd	50	0
Marinara sauce, jarred (any with ≤ 100 calories and ≤ 2 grams of fat per cup)	1 cup	100	2

Figure 2-4

Meal Plan: Dinner Menus

Complete the following assignments before the next session:

☐ *Activity*: Exercise (e.g., brisk walking) for 15 minutes × 3 days.

☐ *Behavior*: Complete the Remember Your Purpose Worksheet (Worksheet 2-2).

☐ *Calories*: Follow a diet that is consistent with your calorie goal (1,200–1,500 for <250 lbs.; 1,500–1,800 for >250 lbs.). Total the calories for each day (and for the week), calculate a seven-day average, and compare results to your target range.

Reduce by one-third or continue to eat a lower intake of high-calorie foods. See the Cutting Back on High Calorie Foods Form (Worksheet 1-1) for examples of high-calorie foods.

☐ *Days Recorded*: Using a copy of the Keeping Track Form, record all the foods and drinks (except for water) that you consume (including the time, amount, type, and description of food). Record every day.

☐ *Experiential Exercise*: N/A

☐ *Reminder*: Complete your Check-In sheet before the next session. Also, don't forget to bring your Keeping Track Forms (or printout that includes foods, time eaten, and calories).

Meal #1: McDonald's

Food/Beverage	Amount	Calories
Burger with cheese	1-quarter pound burger with cheese	520
French fries	1 large serving 5.5 oz	500
Milk Shake	16 oz chocolate shake	705

TOTAL: __1,725__ Calories

Meal # 2: Prepared at Home

Food/Beverage	Amount	Calories
12-grain bread	2 slices	220
Turkey Meat	2 slices Butterball, Sliced, oven-roasted	60
Lettuce	¼ cup shredded	1.75
Tomato	⅓ small raw tomato sliced	5
Mustard	1 tsp	5
Apple	1 medium	75
Milk	1 cup skim 8 oz	90

TOTAL: __456.75__ Calories

Figure 2-5

Calorie Tracking Example Worksheet Answers

Instructions: Complete the following items before you attend Session 3.

A. *Activity*: Last week I exercised on _____ days, for an average of _____ minutes per day.

   (The goal for last week was 3 × 15 minutes of activity.)

B. *Behavior*: I did/did not (circle one) complete the Remember Your Purpose Worksheet.

C. *Calories*: My daily calorie goal was _____ and my daily calorie average was _____.

   I did/did not (circle one) cut back on my intake of high-fat and high-sugar foods by at least one-third.

D. *Days Recorded*: I recorded my intake for _____ of the past seven days.

E. *Experiential Exercise*: N/A

CHAPTER 3

Session 3: Goal Setting; Weighing and Measuring

Goals for This Session

- To review events of the past week and check in about progress
- To set and evaluate weight loss goals
- To learn skills about weighing and measuring
- To discuss assignments for the coming week

Effective Goal Setting

The main goal of this program is to help you achieve a weight loss of 1–2 pounds per week, because that rate of weight loss has been shown to maximize success and safety. (Note that overly rapid weight loss can contribute to later weight regain and can also put you at risk for medical problems such as gallstones.) This program recommends an *initial* goal of a 10% weight reduction. When 10% is reached, another goal can be set based on what makes the most sense for you at that time. Many people do have weight loss goals of more than 10%. Having long-term goals of this type is not a problem, but the program strongly recommends that you start out with a goal of 10% and that you are most focused on week-to-week losses of 1–2 pounds. You can always decide to set a new weight loss goal once you have reached 10% weight loss. Note that having unrealistically large weight loss expectations is associated with losing *less* weight.

Setting Behavioral Goals

1. Goals should be *specific*. Specific goals such as, "Walk two times this week after work on Tuesday and Thursday in the park" are more likely to be accomplished that general ones such as, "Walk more this week." Similarly, "Eat 1,300 calories per day" is more likely to be accomplished than "Eat fewer calories this week."

2. Goals should also be *reasonable,* which means that you should aim to make small changes. If you're not walking at all, do not try to walk every day. The smaller the difference between your current behavior and your goal behavior, the greater the chances you will accomplish it. Small successes lead to big successes.

3. Goals should be *active.* You should define your goals in terms of what *to do* rather than what *not to do.* For example, "Eat every four hours" is better than "Stop going all day without eating" and "Walk after dinner" is better than "Stop lying on the couch after dinner."

4. Goals should also be *short term.* You will assess your goals over short intervals (no more than a week). Sometimes, even shorter intervals are helpful (e.g., day by day). Reviewing your progress after short periods will enable you to assess your accomplishments and trouble-shoot any difficulties.

5. Goals should also be *limited.* For this program, select no more than two goals per week. Selecting more goals will decrease your focus and make adherence more difficult. Once your goals have been accomplished and maintained, you can select new goals.

6. Finally, *record* your progress. It is helpful to keep a written record of your goals and progress each week. The recording process will increase awareness of your goal and provide an accurate record of your progress. The simplest and easiest records work best. Do what works for you.

Weighing and Measuring Foods

Calories are based on amount consumed, so it is extremely important to use measuring utensils and a food scale to *accurately* determine the amount you eat and drink. You need to weigh and measure foods and drinks for *at least two weeks* to train the eye to make estimates. After this initial period, you should periodically check your estimates by weighing and measuring foods again in order to avoid portion size drift.

Things to keep in mind:

- When measuring solid foods with measuring cups or spoons, always level it off before recording. Use a tool such as a knife to make the food in the cup/spoon even with the rim, rather than rounded or heaping. If you don't level, you may be taking in more calories than you think.
- When using a liquid measuring cup, measure from eye level.
- When using a food scale, pay attention to small differences. Small differences on the scale can make a big difference in calories.
- Weigh meats after cooking (meats lose about a quarter of their weight during cooking).

Portion Size Tricks

Many people find portion size estimating tricks to be helpful, including:

- A medium potato = Computer mouse
- An average bagel = Hockey puck
- 1 cup of fruit = Baseball
- 3 oz of meat = Deck of playing cards
- 3 oz of fish = Checkbook
- 1 oz of cheese = 2 dice
- 1 teaspoon of peanut butter = Tip of your thumb
- 1 cup of ice cream/yogurt/veggies = Tennis ball
- 4-inch-diameter waffle or pancake = CD

Skill Builder for Session 3

Complete the following assignments before the next session:

- ☐ *Activity*: Exercise (e.g., brisk walking) for 15 minutes × 3 days. Record type and minutes on your Keeping Track Form.
- ☐ *Behavior*: Weigh and measure all food and drinks except water. On your Keeping Track Forms, mark with an asterisk (*) any times

you were surprised by the number of calories in a food or drink you measured or weighed.

Work on the behavioral goal that you identified during today's session (specify goal here):

_____

_____

_____

Complete the What Meals and Snacks Work for Me Worksheet in Appendix E (Worksheet 3-1).

☐ *Calories*: Follow a diet that is consistent with your calorie goal. Total the calories for each day (and for the week), calculate a seven-day average, and compare results to your calorie target.

Reduce (by one-third) or continue to lower your intake of high-calorie foods.

☐ *Days Recorded*: Record every day.

☐ *Experiential Exercise*: N/A

☐ *Reminder*: Complete your Check-In sheet before the next session. Also, don't forget to bring your Keeping Track Forms (or printout that includes foods, time eaten, and calories).

Instructions: Complete the items below *before* you attend Session 4.

A. *Activity*: Last week I exercised on _____ days, for an average of _____ minutes per day.

(The goal for last week was 3 × 15 minutes of activity.)

B. *Behavior*: I did/did not *(circle one)* weigh and measure all foods and drinks except for water.

The behavioral goal I set in session last week: _____

_____

_____

I did/did not *(circle one)* achieve my behavioral goal.

I did/did not *(circle one)* complete the What Meals and Snacks Work for Me Worksheet.

C. *Calories*: My daily calorie goal was _____ and my daily calorie average was _____.

I did/did not *(circle one)* cut back on my intake of high-fat and high-sugar foods by at least one-third.

D. *Days Recorded*: I recorded my intake for _____ of the past seven days.

E. *Experiential Exercise*: N/A

CHAPTER 4

Session 4: Labels, Planning, and Calorie Accounting

Goals for This Session

- To review events of the past week and check in about progress
- To develop skills in reading nutrition labels
- To review the importance of meal planning
- To introduce methods of accounting for the "cost" of calories
- To discuss assignments for the coming week

Nutrition Labels

When eating packaged foods, it is important to look at the labels to understand how many calories you're taking in. As you can see from the sample nutrition label shown in Figure 4-1, the top of the label tells you the serving size, calories, and fat. You should also pay attention to the total number of servings included in the package.

You may want to also pay attention to the fat, cholesterol, and sodium in each serving. Healthy food choices are generally lower in fat, cholesterol, and sodium content. You may also want to review the ingredient list to learn about the nutrition contained in your food. Look for key phrases like "whole wheat" or "whole oat" listed as the first ingredient for foods that are whole grain. Many foods that say "made with whole grain" on the front of the package are not really 100% whole grain.

Nutrition Facts

Serving Size 1 oz. (28 g/about 19 pieces)
Servings Per Container 8

Amount Per Serving
Calories 140   Calories from Fat 90

                                          % Daily Value*
Total Fat 10 g   15%
  Saturated Fat 2 g   10%
Cholesterol 0 mg   0%
Sodium 384 mg   16%
Total Carbohydrate 16 g   5%
  Dietary Fiber 1 g   1%
  Sugars 1 g
Protein 3 g

Vitamin A 0%   Vitamin C 0%   Calcium 0%   Iron 1%

* Percent Daily Values are based on a 2,000 calorie diet. Your daily values may be higher or lower depending on your calorie needs:

	Calories	2,000	2,500
Total Fat	Less than	65 g	80 g
Sat Fat	Less than	20 g	25 g
Cholesterol	Less than	300 mg	300 mg
Sodium	Less than	2,400 mg	2,40 0 mg
Total Carbohydrate		300 g	375 g
Dietary Fiber		25 g	30 g

Calories per gram:
Fat   9   Carbohydrate 4   Protein 4

Check the **Serving Size** and compare this to how much you ate. Did you have more than one serving?

Look at the **Calories per serving**

If you eat more than the amount listed for one serving you will be eating more calories than the amount on the label.

Figure 4-1

Introduction to Nutrition Labels

The Importance of Meal Planning

There are many benefits to planning meals and snacks. Take a moment to think of some and list them here:

Benefits of planning meals and snacks:

_____

_____

_____

_____

Sometimes challenges to planning can arise. In these cases, it may be helpful to use resources to help you get back on track. Magazines, cookbooks, and websites can all be helpful places to find healthy recipes and ideas for snacks. Tables 4-1 and 4-2 contain resources for healthy eating that you may find helpful.

Table 4-1 Online Resources for Healthy Eating

Resource	Website
Eating Well: Where Good Taste Meets Good Health Menus	http://www.eatingwell.com/recipes_menus/collections
Self: Healthy Meal and Snack Recipes	http://www.self.com/fooddiet/
Livestrong: Diet and Nutrition Resources	http://www.livestrong.com/healthy-eating/
Cooking Light: In-Season Foods, Recipe Finder, Everyday Menus, Quick & Healthy	http://www.cookinglight.com/food/
Meals Matter: Meal Planning Made Simple	http://www.mealsmatter.org/
Food Network: Healthy-Eats	http://www.foodnetwork.com/healthyeating/index.html
Whole Living: Body + Soul in Balance Healthy Snack Recipes	http://www.wholeliving.com/136353/healthy-snack-recipes
Real Simple: Every Day Recipes	http://www.realsimple.com/food-recipes/index.html
Prevention: Healthy Foods	http://www.prevention.com/food/healthy-eating-tips/25-super-healthy-foods
Food.com: Low-Calorie Recipes	http://www.food.com/recipes/low-calorie
Lowfat Lifestyle: Low-Calorie Recipe Index	http://www.lowfatlifestyle.com/recipefolder/recipeindex.htm
Every Day With Rachael Ray: Healthy Snacks	http://www.rachaelraymag.com/recipes/103-healthy-snack-recipe-ideas
Shape: Healthy Recipes & Cooking Ideas	http://www.shape.com/healthy-eating/healthy-recipes
101 Cookbooks, A Recipe Journal: Healthy Recipes by Ingredient	http://www.101cookbooks.com/
ChooseMyPlate.gov: Healthy Meal Planning	http://www.choosemyplate.gov/food-groups/

The next step is to figure out how to fit recipe and snack ideas into a daily plan. Use the Daily Meal Planner Worksheet (Worksheet 4-1) in Appendix E to practice planning. The idea is to come up with a plan that you will follow for the next seven days. This means you will also need to do your grocery shopping based on your meal plan. You may want to look back at Figures 2-2, 2-3, and 2-4 from Chapter 2 for some sample meal plans.

Table 4-2 Written Resources for Healthy Eating

America's Test Kitchen Light & Healthy 2012: The Year's Best Recipes Lightened Up	By Carl Tremblay and Daniel J. Van Ackere, America's Test Kitchen, 2012
The 300 Calorie Cookbook: 300 Tasty Meals for Eating Healthy Every Day	By Betty Crocker Editors, Wiley, 2009
The Biggest Loser Cookbook: More than 125 Healthy, Delicious Recipes Adapted from NBC's Hit Show	By Devin Alexander and Karen Kaplan, Rodale Books, 2006
Spices of Life: Simple and Delicious Recipes for Great Health	By Nina Simonds, Knopf, 2005
The New Mediterranean Diet Cookbook: A Delicious Alternative for Lifelong Health	By Nancy Harmon Jenkins, Bantam, 2009
The Santa Monica Farmers' Market Cookbook: Seasonal Foods, Simple Recipes, and Stories from the Market and Farm	By Amelia Saltsman, Blenheim Press, 2007
Ancient Grains for Modern Meals	By Maria Speck, Ten Speed Press, 2011

Calorie Accounting

Sometimes it's helpful to think of calories the same way you would think of your funds. A calorie account is like a household budget or bank account. You may spend your calories in your account based on your personal preferences, but consider how much you enjoy a particular food versus what it costs calorically. Consider which foods are most satisfying in terms of hunger.

Your calorie balance allows for flexibility. That is, you can save calories for special occasions, just as you save money. For example, to prepare for a special occasion on a Saturday, you could save 100 calories each day, Monday through Friday, to have 500 extra calories to "spend" (use) on Saturday. However, you need to make sure that your goals for any single day are not too low (e.g., not less than approximately 1000 or 1200 calories, depending on energy needs). You can also spend less afterward (after Saturday, in this example), to adjust for an unusually high calorie meal or day.

Many people in this program find it helpful to tally caloric intake as they go through the day. This way, if you overeat on one occasion during the day you can still keep your calorie account balanced by making adjustments at other times you eat. Over the course of a week, your calorie ledger must average to your daily calorie goal.

Skill Builder for Session 4

Complete the following assignments before the next session:

☐ *Activity*: Exercise (e.g., brisk walking) for 15 minutes × 3 days. Record type and minutes on your Keeping Track Form.

☐ *Behavior*: Complete the Daily Meal Planner Worksheet (Worksheet 4-1) and attempt to follow it for the whole week.

☐ *Calories*: Follow a diet that is consistent with your calorie goal. Total the calories for each day (and for the week), calculate a seven-day average, and compare results to your calorie target.

☐ *Days Recorded*: Record every day.

☐ *Experiential Exercise*: N/A

☐ *Reminder*: Complete your Check-In sheet before the next session. Also, don't forget to bring your Keeping Track Forms (or printout that includes foods, time eaten, and calories).

Instructions: Complete the items below *before* you attend Session 5.

A. *Activity*: Last week I exercised on _____ days, for an average of _____ minutes per day.

(The goal for last week was 3 × 15 minutes of activity.)

B. *Behavior*: I did/did not *(circle one)* complete the Daily Meal Planner Worksheet and attempt to follow it for the whole week.

C. *Calories*: My daily calorie goal was _____ and my daily calorie average was _____.

D. *Days Recorded*: I recorded my intake for _____ of the past seven days.

E. *Experiential Exercise*: N/A

CHAPTER 5

Session 5: Control What You Can, Accept What You Can't; The Home Food Environment

Goals for This Session

- To review events of the past week and check in about progress
- To differentiate between things that can and can't be controlled during weight loss and introduce the importance of accepting things that are outside of one's control
- To learn how to control challenges to weight control at home
- To discuss assignments for the coming week

Control What You Can, Accept What You Can't

In this program, we address challenges of losing weight—and keeping it off—that many other programs neglect. Many people trying to lose weight have reported that they have been able to change their eating and/ or physical activity behaviors in the short term, but it became difficult to maintain those changes, and they eventually fell back into their old habits. This may have been the case with you as well.

Science has shown that weight loss, and especially weight maintenance, is made difficult by our biology and the environment. There is no "magic bullet" that any weight loss program can offer that will make long-term weight loss effortless. Human bodies are biologically hard-wired to desire high-calorie foods. During evolution, we developed an attraction to good tasting foods, because it helped us survive. Similarly, over long periods of human history we developed a preference to avoid expending energy (i.e., exercising) unnecessarily.

To make the problem worse, we in the Western world are surrounded by high-calorie foods that are very easily available. In fact, we live in an "obesogenic" food environment, meaning that the unhealthy food around us pushes us to overeat and therefore to become overweight. We can find examples of unhealthy food almost anywhere, such as in supermarket displays, on restaurant dishes at the next table, the box of donuts in a conference room, or a tray of ziti at a neighbor's party. Most of us also do not burn enough calories in our day-to-day lives, so it takes a concerted effort (i.e., "exercise") to compensate for our sedentary lifestyles.

Most weight loss programs do not address the biology and environmental problem. This program does. Specifically, it acknowledges that we all exist in an environment that is constantly triggering our hardwired desire to get pleasure from food and from rest. We focus on new ways to respond to these challenges and problems—ways that are different from how you may have responded in the past.

This program will teach you to:

1. Establish good habits so that you don't have to make difficult decisions as often (i.e., how you can help healthy behavior to happen automatically and become habit).
2. Train your mind to be successful at long-term lifestyle change by:

   (a) Becoming more accepting of the less comfortable, rather than the most comfortable, psychological state (e.g., choosing to go to the gym rather than staying on the couch and watching TV, choosing the less pleasurable food that is in the calorie range rather than choosing the more tempting food option).
   (b) Becoming more willing to choose behaviors that are consistent with your most important life values, even if doing so produces a less comfortable/less pleasurable psychological state. Examples include prioritizing time to exercise, even when you're tired, because you value being an active person and a good role model for your kids; eating fruit for a snack rather than chips because

you value your health and know the high levels of sodium in chips are against your doctor's recommendations.

(c) Clarify the values by which you would like to, and will come to, live your life.

(d) Keep these values front and center and not slip into mindless behavior that you will likely end up regretting.

(e) Become able to sustain long-term commitment to behavior change.

The overarching framework of our program is *"Control what you can, accept what you can't."* This framework holds that:

- Our *behaviors* are within our control.
- However, even after enacting many weight control behaviors, *challenges* remain.
- A willingness to *accept* these difficulties is necessary for long-term success.
- Note: Acceptance of *internal experiences* and *our obesogenic environment* does *not* mean an acceptance of *behavior* that runs counter to weight control.

Table 5-1 gives examples of things that you can control and things that you must accept.

Table 5-1 Control What You Can, Accept What You Can't

What You Can Control	What You Must Accept
<ul><li>Your behaviors<ul><li>Recording calories</li><li>Planning meals</li><li>Stocking your home with low-calorie foods and getting rid of high-calorie foods</li><li>Eating regularly</li><li>Staying within calorie goals</li><li>Engaging in physical activity</li><li>Reducing portion sizes</li></ul></li></ul>	<ul><li>Obesogenic environment<ul><li>High-calorie, delicious foods (actual foods and images of foods)</li><li>Labor-saving devices</li></ul></li><li>Your internal experiences<ul><li>Urges to eat</li><li>Desire to be comfortable</li><li>Cravings</li><li>Your mind coming up with reasons for overeating or avoiding exercise</li><li>Anxiety</li><li>Sadness</li><li>Fatigue</li><li>Muscle soreness</li></ul></li></ul>

As mentioned in the last session, one of the reasons it is so hard to lose weight and maintain these losses is because we live in an environment where there is an abundance of high-calorie, delicious foods that are very easy to obtain.

Set yourself up for success by making it more difficult to have high-calorie foods, especially those that you find hard to eat in moderation. In other words, reduce the availability of and access to foods that are tempting.

1. *Remove* these foods from your home (e.g., throw them out, donate them, give food to others).
2. *Do not continue to purchase* these foods.
3. Stock up your home with *low-calorie* options.
4. Put *higher calorie foods* in the *back* of the fridge/cabinets, and put *lower calorie items* toward the *front*.

In the following space, describe one specific change that you will make in your home environment this week:

_____

_____

_____

_____

Skill Builder for Session 5

Complete the following assignments before the next session:

☐ *Activity*: Exercise (e.g., brisk walking) for 15 minutes × 3 days. Record type and minutes on your Keeping Track Form.

☐ *Behavior*: (1) Practice using the Calorie Accounting principles to keep track of calories each day. Mark on your Keeping Track Form instances in which you "banked" calories. (2) Make at least one change in your home or work environment.

☐ *Calories*: Follow a diet that is consistent with your calorie goal. Total the calories for each day (and for the week), calculate a seven-day average, and compare results to your calorie target.

☐ *Days Recorded*: Record every day.

☐ *Experiential Exercise*: Complete the Control What You Can, Accept What You Can't Worksheet in Appendix E (Worksheet 5-1).[1]

☐ *Reminder*: Complete your Check-In sheet before the next session. Also, don't forget to bring your Keeping Track Forms (or printout that includes foods, time eaten, and calories).

---

[1]Starting this week we will be collecting your written assignments to provide feedback.

Instructions: Complete the following items *before* you attend Session 6.

A. *Activity*: Last week I exercised on _____ days, for an average of _____ minutes per day.

(The goal for last week was 3 × 15 minutes of activity.)

B. *Behavior*: (1) I did/did not *(circle one)* practice calorie accounting, and I did/did not *(circle one)* mark times I "banked" calories on my Keeping Track Forms. (2) I did/did not *(circle one)* make at least one change in my home or work environment.

C. *Calories*: My daily calorie goal was _____ and my daily calorie average was _____.

D. *Days Recorded*: I recorded my intake for _____ of the past seven days.

E. *Experiential Exercise*: I did/did not *(circle one)* complete the Control What You Can, Accept What You Can't Worksheet.

CHAPTER 6

Session 6: Physical Activity and Willingness (Part 1)

Goals for This Session

- To review events of the past week and check in about progress
- To discuss the benefits of increasing your level of physical activity
- To review the activity progression for the remainder of the program and discuss methods for scheduling activity
- To discuss the concept of willingness in the context of weight control
- To discuss assignments for the coming week

Benefits of Physical Activity

Medical, psychological, and weight-control benefits of physical activity include the following:

A. Medical

1. Decreased death risk
2. Reduced risk of coronary artery disease
3. Decreased blood pressure
4. Increased good cholesterol
5. Increased heart strength
6. Decreased risk of osteoporosis
7. Improved diabetes (insulin sensitivity)

8. Associated with long-term weight control
9. Increased energy
10. Need less sleep

B. Psychological

1. Reduced stress, depression
2. Improved self-esteem and body image
3. Part of healthy lifestyle and being good to oneself

C. Weight

1. Not strongly associated with short-term weight loss; it does burn calories, but not enough to produce large weight losses in the short term
2. Exercise, however, is the best predictor of maintenance of weight loss
3. There is a long-term cumulative effect of exercise; it is believed to be the most important factor for long-term weight loss maintenance

Planning Physical Activity

The eventual goal for the program is to reach the equivalent of 250 minutes of aerobic activity per week. This week's goal is to reach a total of 60 minutes of activity (e.g., at least three days for 20 minutes). Activity should be in bouts of at least 10 minutes to count toward your activity goals. Refer to the Activity Goals Worksheet (Worksheet 6-1) to see the activity progression for the next six months of this program. It's very important to keep a daily log of activity using the exercise log, which is part of the Keeping Track Forms. You can also use the Activity Planner Worksheet (Worksheet 6-2) to practice planning out your activity for the upcoming week.

Introduction to Willingness

Experiencing challenges when working on weight control is inevitable. As mentioned before, there is no "magic bullet" that will make long-term weight management effortless.

Willingness = *engaging in weight control behaviors even when it is challenging (i.e., causes less pleasure or even discomfort). Willingness is the alternative to saying, "I'm only going to engage in these behaviors when it's comfortable or easy."*

Here are two examples of willingness in action:

- Walking up to a table of fruits and potato chips. Choosing to eat a piece of fruit, even though you believe that eating chips would bring you more pleasure.
- Walking for 15 more minutes even when you feel tired and are imagining how nice it would be to lie down on the couch and watch TV.

Transforming Your "*Only If . . .*" Responses to "*Even If . . .*" Responses

At this point in the program, it is important for you to decide what you are willing to experience with respect to weight management efforts. Examine your level of *willingness* to engage in weight control behaviors by identifying one or two "only if" thoughts that you have in the blank spaces in Worksheet 6-4 and transforming them to "even if" responses. "Only if" statements imply that we are only willing to engage in weight control behaviors under certain conditions. "Even if" statements indicate that we are committed to engaging in weight control behaviors regardless of the conditions or circumstances (i.e., regardless of how comfortable it may feel).

The skill you'll practice for this week is noticing instances of "only if" responding and changing them to "even if" responding using Worksheet 6-5 at home. Note that Worksheet 6-5 is similar to 6-4 but is not identical. You will use Worksheet 6-5 to record times when you practiced changing "only if" to "even if" responding over the next week.

Skill Builder for Session 6

Complete the following assignments before the next session:

- ☐ *Activity*: Exercise (e.g., brisk walking) for 20 minutes × 3 days (note that this is an increase from last session). Record type and minutes on your Keeping Track Form.

- [ ] *Behavior*: Finish the Activity Planner Worksheet (Worksheet 6-2) that you began during group and follow your Activity Planner for the upcoming week. Read the Types of Exercise Worksheet (Worksheet 6-3).

- [ ] *Calories*: Follow a diet that is consistent with your calorie goal. Total the calories for each day (and for the week), calculate a seven-day average, and compare results to your calorie target.

- [ ] *Days Recorded*: Record all foods and beverages consumed (including the time of eating, the amount and type of food, and the calorie content of all items).

- [ ] *Experiential Exercise*: Complete the Transforming "Only If . . ." Responses to "Even If . . ." Responses at Home Worksheet (Worksheet 6-5).[1]

- [ ] *Reminder*: Complete your Check-In sheet before the next session. Also, don't forget to bring your Keeping Track Forms (or printout that includes foods, time eaten, and calories).

---

[1]Reminder: We will be collecting these at the next group.

Instructions: Complete the following items *before* you attend Session 7.

A. *Activity*: Last week I exercised on _____ days, for an average of _____ minutes per day.

(The goal for last week was 3 × 20 minutes of activity.)

B. *Behavior*: I did/did not *(circle one)* complete the Activity Planner, and I did/did not *(circle one)* follow my Activity Planner for the week. I did/did not *(circle one)* read the Types of Exercise Worksheet.

C. *Calories*: My daily calorie goal was _____ and my daily calorie average was _____.

D. *Days Recorded*: I recorded my intake for _____ of the past seven days.

E. *Experiential Exercise*: I did/did not *(circle one)* complete the Transforming "Only If . . ." Responses to "Even If . . ." Responses at Home Worksheet.

CHAPTER 7

Session 7: Willingness (Part 2) and Values

Goals for This Session

- To review events of the past week and check in about progress
- To learn additional strategies for increasing your willingness to experience uncomfortable thoughts, feelings, and urges that may arise as you try to meet your weight loss goals
- To introduce the concept of values
- To discuss assignments for the coming week

Willingness, Part 2

Willingness is the extent to which you are willing to have whatever thoughts and feelings that you have and still engage in desired behaviors. For example, imagine you have a choice of whether to eat some carrot sticks and stay within your calorie goal, or to eat a chocolate bar and go over your goal. If you are willing to have thoughts such as "I need to eat that chocolate," "I deserve to eat the chocolate," and "Carrots don't taste good" and *still* engage in the healthy behaviors of eating the carrot and passing on the chocolate, you are practicing being willing. Willingness is a skill that takes repeated practice. This week, you will use the Practicing Willingness Worksheet (Worksheet 7-1) to begin developing this skill.

Values are the ideas, principles, and domains in your life that are most precious to you. They can serve as guideposts for behavior and represent what you want your life to be about. Values are the ultimate explanation of your freely chosen behavior.

Values Versus Goals

Values are different from goals. *Goals* are like "mile-markers," or things you can aim to achieve or surpass. For example, you can pass mile-marker 84 on the highway and then proceed toward other mile-markers. A value is the direction in which you are going, or something that you are always moving toward.

Values are not something that you "accomplish" but rather something you consistently aspire to throughout your life. Values cannot be obtained; rather, they describe how you want to live your life. For example, if you value being a devoted parent, you cannot simply give time and attention to your children for a few months and consider being a devoted parent to be completed. Similarly, weight loss can be a goal, but a value is the reason why weight loss is important to you.

Values Versus Feelings

Values are not things that you can have in the way that you have a feeling. *Feelings* are often transient, while values are things that you choose as important and that you constantly work toward.

Feelings often cannot be controlled. Choosing to live your life in a certain direction, or according to a certain value, is something you can control. So "happiness" (a feeling) cannot be a value; when you choose behaviors that move you toward your value, you might feel happy, but the feeling is separate from the value.

Why Values Matter

Values serve not only as a compass for behavior but they also provide the reason *willingness* is worth it. Losing weight and keeping it off can be uncomfortable. Values are the reason it's worth it to you to lose weight anyway.

Now it's time to figure out what is important to you—what your values are. Using the 10 Valued Domains Worksheet (Worksheet 7-2), write down 10 reasons you value developing healthy eating and activity behaviors.

Skill Builder for Session 7

Complete the following assignments before the next session:

☐ *Activity*: Exercise (e.g., brisk walking) for 20 minutes × 3 days. Record type and minutes on your Keeping Track Form.

☐ *Behavior*: Work on the behavioral goal that you identified during today's session (specify goal here):

_____

_____

_____

☐ *Calories*: Follow a diet that is consistent with your calorie goal. Total the calories for each day (and for the week), calculate a seven-day average, and compare results to your calorie target.

☐ *Days Recorded*: Record every day.

☐ *Experiential Exercise*: Using the Practicing Willingness Worksheet (Worksheet 7-1), record any relevant thoughts/feelings/urges that come up this week, rate your willingness on a scale of 1 to 10, and write down the final behavior that resulted. Also complete the 10 Valued Domains Worksheet (Worksheet 7-2).

☐ *Reminder*: Complete your Check-In sheet before the next session. Also, don't forget to bring your Keeping Track Forms (or printout that includes foods, time eaten, and calories).

Instructions: Complete the following items *before* you attend Session 8.

A. *Activity*: Last week I exercised on _____ days, for an average of _____ minutes per day.

(The goal for last week was 3 × 20 minutes of activity.)

B. *Behavior*: The behavioral goal I set in session last week:

_____

_____

_____

I did/did not *(circle one)* achieve my behavioral goal.

C. *Calories*: My daily calorie goal was _____ and my daily calorie average was _____.

D. *Days Recorded*: I recorded my intake for _____ of the past seven days.

E. *Experiential Exercise*: I did/did not *(circle one)* complete the Practicing Willingness Worksheet, and I did/did not *(circle one)* complete the 10 Valued Domains Worksheet.

CHAPTER 8

Session 8: Forming Good Habits and Flexibility

Goals for This Session

- To review events of the past week and check in about progress
- To gain further clarity about your values
- To learn how forming positive habits can help with weight control
- To learn why flexibility in behaviors can help in achieving weight loss goals and introduce pattern smashing
- To discuss assignments for the coming week

Values Clarity

Values are important because they help you decide how you want to live. However, we often don't take the time to think deeply about our values. Here are some questions to ponder:

- What ideas should make life worth living and tell you what decisions to make?
- If you were at the end of your life looking back, what would you hope were the principles that shaped your life?
- When you engage in difficult behaviors, what are the underlying reasons that it is *worth it* to experience discomforts like boredom, anxiety, and tiredness?

Not all values will be directly relevant to healthy eating and physical activity; however, many will be. Think about your answers to the previous questions and the worksheet you completed. Which of these values connect to your health goals?

Forming Good Habits and Breaking Out of Bad Ones

Habits can work both for and against your weight control efforts.

Forming Good Habits

Forming good habits is often much more effective than attempting to make a difficult decision over and over again. If we had to decide whether or not to brush our teeth every night, we probably wouldn't on many nights. But if it is a habit, we just automatically do it without thinking. By practicing a behavior so many times that your brain no longer thinks about it, it is possible to establish positive healthy habits.

Here are some suggestions for establishing good habits:

1. Perform the behavior after a "cue" like a time (right after waking up) or event (after dinner).
2. Start with behavior that is extremely likely. (When you wake up, put on your walking clothes, go outside, and enjoy the fresh air for five minutes. Don't actually take a walk.) Then gradually shift the behavior so that it increasingly resembles the behavior goal.
3. Repeat the behavior after the cue for 30 days in a row.

Breaking Bad Habits

Narrowness Versus Flexibility

Narrowness refers to always responding the same way to the same thoughts, feelings, or situations. Being unwilling to have thoughts/feelings/sensations/loss of pleasure that arise from different choices narrows our behavioral options. *Flexibility* refers to the ability to break out of bad habits. Being willing to have an experience even when it is less pleasurable or uncomfortable gives us more flexibility in terms of how we can behave. For example, narrowness might mean that every time you get home from work and are tired, you sit on the couch and watch television. This has become a habit. Flexibility might mean getting home from work and feeling tired, but choosing to do something else instead, like going for a walk.

Like willingness and several other concepts that have been discussed, flexibility is a skill that takes practice. This week, you will use the Practicing Flexibility Worksheet (Worksheet 8-1) to begin developing the skill of behaving flexibly.

Building Flexibility: Pattern Smashing

Most individuals have developed narrow habits in response to specific thoughts, feelings, and situations. These problematic behaviors are *not mindfully chosen*, are often *not helpful,* and can make weight control *difficult*. One way to respond to these problematic behaviors and build flexibility is *pattern smashing*.

Pattern Smashing = Deliberately engaging in behavior that runs counter to your old pattern of behavior.

- Pattern smashing is critical for weight control because *old patterns* of behavior were *not working*.
- When certain internal experiences always lead to choosing certain behaviors that go against your weight control goals, you should pattern smash.

Examples of pattern smashing:

- If you always have dessert after dinner, skip dessert one night.
- If you always skip exercise when it is raining outside, exercise inside instead.
- If you always drink a glass of wine when eating out, select a different low-calorie beverage instead.

Skill Builder for Session 8

Complete the following assignments before the next session:

☐ *Activity*: Exercise (e.g., brisk walking) for 20 minutes × 4 days (which is an increase from last session). Record type and minutes on your Keeping Track Form.

☐ *Behavior*: Complete the Practicing Flexibility Worksheet (Worksheet 8-1) and practice different ways of behaving in response to the same situation.

☐ *Calories*: Follow a diet that is consistent with your calorie goal. Total the calories for each day (and for the week), calculate a seven-day average, and compare results to your calorie target.

☐ *Days Recorded*: Record every day.

☐ *Experiential Exercise*: Complete the Pattern Smashing Activity (Worksheet 8-2).

☐ *Reminder*: Complete your Check-In sheet before the next session. Also, don't forget to bring your Keeping Track Forms (or printout that includes foods, time eaten, and calories).

Instructions: Complete the items below *before* you attend Session 8.

A. *Activity*: Last week I exercised on _____ days, for an average of _____ minutes per day.

(The goal for last week was 4 × 20 minutes of activity.)

B. *Behavior*: I did/did not *(circle one)* complete the Practicing Flexibility Worksheet.

C. *Calories*: My daily calorie goal was _____ and my daily calorie average was _____.

D. *Days Recorded*: I recorded my intake for _____ of the past seven days.

E. *Experiential Exercise*: I did/did not *(circle one)* complete the Pattern Smashing Activity.

CHAPTER 9

Session 9: Restaurant Eating; Handling Weekends and Special Occasions

- To review events of the past week and check in about progress
- To learn new ways to stick to calorie goals when eating out at restaurants
- To discuss eating and physical activity on weekends and holidays
- To discuss assignments for the coming week

Restaurant Eating

Restaurant eating is a particularly challenging type of eating situation for weight control behaviors. The first and best strategy is to eat out as little as possible. Restaurants are full of tempting choices, and most people cannot resist these temptations and end up breaking their calorie goals.

When you do eat out, however, there are several strategies that you can use to make healthy choices. Strategies to assist you in eating healthy while dining out are listed on the Restaurant Eating Tips Worksheet (Worksheet 9-1).

Handling Weekends

Do you find it hard to eat less and stay active on weekends? Here are some tips:

1. Plan ahead.

    - A lack of structure can make weekends a challenge.
    - Instead, plan what you will eat and when.
    - Plan how you will be active and when.
    - Include a back-up plan. For instance, what if you're too busy shopping to get home for lunch? Plan and prepare a healthy lunch to bring with you.
    - What if your friends ask you to eat out on Saturday night? Plan to eat half and bring the rest home in a doggie bag.

2. Incorporate pleasures and events that are not food related.

    - Many of us use the weekend to do chores or errands.
    - But you should also plan times to relax during the weekend.
    - Think about how being active could be a fun part of the weekend.

3. Don't skip meals.

    - It may be tempting to sleep late and skip breakfast on weekends, or you may be so busy running errands that you skip lunch.
    - Skipping meals can lead you to eat too much later in the day.
    - It will also cause low blood sugar.
    - Instead, plan quick meals and snacks. For instance, drink some low-fat milk and have a piece of fruit and toast when you get up. Pack an apple or a hard-boiled egg before you leave home to run errands. You'll have them on hand if you can't eat lunch on time.

Handling Vacations/Holidays

Vacations and holidays are a time to escape from everyday work and family responsibilities and to indulge in more pleasurable activities. Because eating is also a pleasurable activity, many of us may be inclined to revert to old, unconstructive habits, including eating high-calorie foods and not exercising. Here are some of ideas for staying on track during these special occasions:

1. Incorporate pleasures and rewards that are not food or drink related.

   - What do you want your vacation or holiday to be like?
   - Think about how being active could be a fun part of the holiday (e.g., a hike or walk in the park).

2. Bring your family/friends on board with your goals for the vacation or holiday.

   - "How do we want our vacation to look similar or different to previous vacations?"
   - "Let's find ways make good food choices even if we choose to eat out."
   - "What are some fun ways to work exercise into our vacation?"
   - Talk about concrete ways your friends or family can help you with your food/eating goals on your vacation, including what to say and not to say.

3. Set expectations you can meet for your vacation or holiday.

   - Continue to monitor your eating and activity.
   - Weigh yourself weekly. (But remember, there might be small differences between scales.)
   - Eat something special. (Choose an exotic dish.)
   - Think about setting a weight maintenance versus a weight loss goal while on vacation.
   - Get in extra activity.

4. Make time for yourself while on vacation or during holidays.

   - Assert yourself so that you are not always doing what others want to do.
   - Vacations are often busy; find time to relax.

5. Plan ahead regarding alcohol.

   - Alcohol often impairs your ability to control your eating optimally.
   - Remember that calories from alcohol add up quickly.

6. Relax, but be active!

   ■   Look for ways to be active that you enjoy.

7. Prepare for comments regarding your weight from family/friends.

Here are a few additional tips for holidays:

■ Plan ahead of time what you will eat at a holiday meal.
■ Have conversations ahead of time with family members and friends asking for the support that you need.
■ Plan ahead of time what you will say to others who remark on your eating.
■ Bank calories.

Skill Builder for Session 9

Complete the following assignments before the next session:

☐ *Activity*: Exercise (e.g., brisk walking) for 20 minutes × 4 days. Record type and minutes on your Keeping Track Form.

☐ *Behavior*: (1) Read the Restaurant Eating Tips Worksheet (Worksheet 9-1). When eating out this week, identify and practice key strategies from the worksheet to help you stay within your calorie goal. (2) Identify and implement a specific behavioral strategy for handling weekends.

☐ *Calories*: Follow a diet that is consistent with your calorie goal. Total the calories for each day (and for the week), calculate a seven-day average, and compare results to your calorie target.

☐ *Days Recorded*: Record every day.

☐ *Experiential Exercise*: N/A

☐ *Reminder*: Complete your Check-In sheet before the next session. Also, don't forget to bring your Keeping Track Forms (or printout that includes foods, time eaten, and calories).

Instructions: Complete the items below *before* you attend Session 10.

A. *Activity*: Last week I exercised on _____ days, for an average of _____ minutes per day.

(The goal for last week was 4 × 20 minutes of activity.)

B. *Behavior*: I did/did not *(circle one)* practice using strategies from the Restaurant Eating Tips Worksheet when eating out, and I did/did not *(circle one)* identify and implement a specific behavioral strategy for handling weekends.

C. *Calories*: My daily calorie goal was _____ and my daily calorie average was _____.

D. *Days Recorded*: I recorded my intake for _____ of the past seven days.

E. *Experiential Exercise*: N/A

CHAPTER 10

Session 10: Barriers to Living a Valued Life

Goals for This Session

- To review events of the past week and check in about progress
- To discuss barriers to living according to values and strategies to overcome them
- To discuss assignments for the coming week

Barriers to Living a Valued Life

Living a life according to your values can be difficult! There are several main reasons we tend to have trouble living according to our values, including not having our values in mind, struggling to remember the long-term benefit if we have to sacrifice short-term reward, and having more than one value that seems to conflict. See Table 10-1 for a list of these challenges and ways to combat them.

Living according to your values will take deliberate practice and willingness to experience discomfort. Use Worksheet 10-1 to practice living according to your values this week. Pay attention to what you needed to be willing to experience, particularly when you needed to combat some of these challenges to living a valued life.

Table 10-1 Barriers to Living a Valued Life and Strategies to Combat Them

Challenge	Strategies to Combat Challenge
Not having values in mind: It is easy to get wrapped up in our daily lives and forget about the things we care about most.	▪ Create written or visual reminders of what you value. Posting notes or pictures in places you'll see can help you to keep your values in mind throughout the day. ▪ Explicitly consider your values every time you make an eating or physical activity decision. *Make every decision a deliberate up or down vote on a value.*
Short-term vs. long-term mind: Our brains often value short-term reward (like tasting a delicious food) more than long-term reward (like losing weight).	▪ Remind yourself that the short term is *very* short (maybe seconds). ▪ Remind yourself that the long term matters a lot more than the short term. ▪ Practice making long-term decisions that trump short-term gains.
Values can seem to conflict with each other.	▪ Work on balance. Try to minimize black-and-white thinking by recognizing that, some days, one value may trump another, but you can prioritize the one that was put on the backburner the next day. ▪ Think flexibly about how to move in the direction of your values. There is more than one way to live out a value. If you are open to new ideas, you may find that your values and living a healthy life do not necessarily conflict. ▪ Think about whichever value you are *not* living out, and mindfully remind yourself of the cost of not living according to this value. What are you missing out on?

Skill Builder for Session 10

Complete the following assignments before the next session:

☐ *Activity*: Exercise (e.g., brisk walking) for 25 minutes × 4 days (which is an increase from last session). Record type and minutes on your Keeping Track Form.

☐ *Behavior*: Work on the behavioral goal that you identified during today's session (specify goal here):

_____

_____

_____

☐ *Calories*: Follow a diet that is consistent with your calorie goal. Total the calories for each day (and for the week), calculate a seven-day average, and compare results to your calorie target.

☐ *Days Recorded*: Record every day.

☐ *Experiential Exercise*: Complete the In Order to Behave Consistently With My Values, I Was Willing to . . . Worksheet (Worksheet 10-1).

☐ *Reminder*: Complete your Check-In sheet before the next session. Also, don't forget to bring your Keeping Track Forms (or printout that includes foods, time eaten, and calories).

Instructions: Complete the items below *before* you attend Session 11.

A. *Activity*: Last week I exercised on _____ days, for an average of _____ minutes per day.

   (The goal for last week was 4 × 25 minutes of activity.)

B. *Behavior*: The behavioral goal I set in session last week:

   _____

   _____

   _____

   I did/did not *(circle one)* achieve my behavioral goal.

C. *Calories*: My daily calorie goal was _____ and my daily calorie average was _____.

D. *Days Recorded*: I recorded my intake for _____ of the past seven days.

E. *Experiential Exercise*: I did/did not *(circle one)* complete the In Order to Behave Consistently With My Values, I Was Willing to … Worksheet.

CHAPTER 11

Session 11: Friends and Family

Goals for This Session

- To review events of the past week and check in about progress
- To discuss the importance of social support and learn how to ask for it
- To discuss how to deal with challenging social situations that can make it difficult to stick to your weight control goals
- To discuss assignments for the coming week

Social Support

Let's switch gears and consider another aspect of your weight control that matters: social support. Family, friends, neighbors, and other people from this program can create challenges or provide help for your weight control efforts. Consider the social influences listed in Tables 11-1 and 11-2 and come up with examples from your own life.

Because others can influence your weight control efforts, it's important that you are able to ask for the support you need. The following are several principles to help guide those conversations:

- *Emphasizing health can help.* Full disclosure of your weight loss efforts is not always necessary. In some cases, you may prefer to ask for support for "healthier eating," "being more active," or "having a

Table 11-1 Challenging Social Influences

Influence	Example
The sight of other people eating high-calorie foods or being inactive.	*Your child eats ice cream in front of you.*
Being offered (or pressured to eat) high-calorie foods or invited to do something inactive.	
Being nagged about your weight control efforts.	
Hearing complaints (or assuming them) regarding your weight control efforts.	

healthier lifestyle," as opposed to "dieting" or "weight loss." Few can argue with a goal of having a healthier lifestyle!

- *Avoid assumptions.* Do not assume that a family member, friend, or coworker knows what to do or not do in order to create an environment that will support weight control efforts.
- *Be specific.* Be as concrete as possible when asking someone to change his or her behavior. Specify who, what, when, where, and how.
- *Acknowledge the support you receive.* Show and tell others that you appreciate the ways they are supporting your efforts to eat a healthy diet and be physically active.
- *Practice being assertive about your needs.* It takes time to get in the habit of changing a behavior, like saying "no" after many years of saying "yes" to food offers. Practice saying "no" in a gentle, but firm manner, and it will become a new habit with time.

Table 11-2 Helpful Social Influences

Influence	Example
The sight of other people eating healthy foods or being active.	*Your spouse walks on the treadmill.*
Being offered healthy foods or invited to do something active.	
Being praised for your weight control efforts.	
Hearing compliments related to your weight control efforts.	

Table 11-3 Ways to Support Weight Control Efforts

Ways to Help Me Eat Healthy:	Ways to Help Me Be More Active:
▪ Serve low-calorie foods for meals.	▪ Go for a walk with me. Or do other physical activities with me.
▪ Don't tempt me with high-calorie foods as a reward or gift.	▪ Plan social events around being active.
▪ Clear the table and put food away as soon as the meal is over.	▪ Compromise when my being active conflicts with our schedule.
▪ Don't offer me second helpings.	▪ Praise me when I do my scheduled activity. Be kind when I don't.
▪ Encourage me to cook new foods.	▪ Provide childcare for me so I can take a walk.
▪ Praise my efforts to eat healthier foods.	▪ Set up a regular date with me to be active.
▪ Other:	▪ Other:

▪ *Use willingness skills.* Willingness can allow you to talk to family or a friend about how to be more supportive of weight control efforts despite discomfort or anxiety.

Consider what type of support you would like to ask for. Table 11-3 lists ideas for what types of support you might request of someone else.

Dealing With Problematic Social Situations

In Table 11-1 you listed some examples of social influences that can be challenging to your weight control efforts. The following steps can help when you are faced with difficult social situations in the future:

1. *Stay away from the challenging social cues whenever possible.* For example, avoid chatting with the people at a party who you think will try to persuade you to eat.
2. *Change the cue.* For example, talk to your spouse about your weight control goals and ask him or her not to suggest going out for fast food on the weekends. You can also tell you coworkers that you are on a weight loss program, and they will be a lot less likely to suggest eating high-calorie foods.

3. *Practice responding in a healthier way.* For example, practice saying "no" to food offers or come up with an easy script to use when people pressure you into eating high-calorie foods. Find a way to phrase your current weight loss effort that you feel comfortable saying, for example, "I'm on a weight loss program and I'm being very careful about what I eat." Try a few out until you find one you like. The more you tell people, the most comfortable and confident you will feel about your weight loss efforts.

Skill Builder for Session 11

Complete the following assignments before the next session:

☐ *Activity*: Exercise (e.g., brisk walking) for 25 minutes × 4 days. Record type and minutes on your Keeping Track Form.

☐ *Behavior*: Practice asking for help in your weight control efforts from a family member, friend, or coworker.

☐ *Calories*: Follow a diet that is consistent with your calorie goal. Total the calories for each day (and for the week), calculate a seven-day average, and compare results to your calorie target.

☐ *Days Recorded*: Record every day.

☐ *Experiential Exercise*: N/A

☐ *Reminder*: Complete your Check-In sheet before the next session. Also, don't forget to bring your Keeping Track Forms (or printout that includes foods, time eaten, and calories).

Instructions: Complete the items below *before* you attend Session 12.

A. *Activity*: Last week I exercised on _____ days, for an average of _____ minutes per day.

(The goal for last week was 4×25 minutes of activity.)

B. *Behavior*: I did/did not *(circle one)* practice asking for help in my weight control efforts from a family member, friend, or coworker.

C. *Calories*: My daily calorie goal was _____ and my daily calorie average was _____.

D. *Days Recorded*: I recorded my intake for _____ of the past seven days.

E. *Experiential Exercise*: N/A

CHAPTER 12 | Session 12: Introduction to Defusion and Urge Surfing

Goals for This Session

- To review events of the past week and check in about progress
- To discuss the concept of defusion
- To review the concept of acceptance and learn how to use urge surfing to facilitate acceptance of uncomfortable internal experiences
- To discuss assignments for the coming week

Introduction to Defusion

Defusion is a state of distance from internal experiences like thoughts, feelings, and sensations. Defusion is seeing those experiences for what they are—just momentary activity in your brain.

Remember these metaphors to help you understand defusion:

- *Hands over face metaphor.* Put your hands over your face. When you have your hand over your face, what do you see? Probably just your skin color, some light, and maybe a line or two. Once you start to pull your hand away from your face though, you can see the outline of your hand, the lines on your hand, or other details. That is an example of moving to defusion. Like moving your hand away from your face, defusion allows you to see your thoughts, feelings, and sensations for what they are—just internal experiences.

- *Yellow sunglasses metaphor.* If you were wearing yellow-tinted sunglasses all day, eventually the world would look like it was tinted yellow, and your brain would start to experience that as reality. If you took the glasses away and held them out from your face, you would be able to see that the world was not tinted yellow, but that the glasses made it seem that way. Fusion is like wearing yellow sunglasses; your thoughts, feelings, and sensations make the world look a certain way, and your brain processes that as reality. Defusion allows you to take those thoughts, feelings, and sensations and hold them out so that you can see they are just internal experiences; they don't define reality.

- *Leaves on a stream metaphor.* Imagine you were a very small insect sitting on a leaf that is floating down a stream. You would see the color green and possibly blue and white up in the sky, and you might feel like you're moving. If you flew away from that leaf up to a tree, you would see many leaves floating down the stream. When you were sitting on that one leaf, your whole reality was just green, blue, white, and movement. From up in the tree, however, you can see leaves floating, the stream, the bank of the stream, and probably many other things. Defusion is getting distance from that one leaf—that represents a thought, feeling, or sensation—and recognizing it for what it is. It is just one experience of many, and it does not define your ultimate reality.

Our brains are programmed to respond in certain ways to cues, so those thoughts, feelings, and sensations are often predictable; for example, seeing a certain food and then having a craving for it. Defusion allows you to see that craving as simply a product of your mind, rather than seeing it as an all-consuming truth (which would probably lead you to eat that food!).

Defusion is a key skill for willingness because it allows you to choose a behavior independent of your internal experiences. When you're fused with your thoughts, feelings, and sensations, you tend to act on them automatically. *Fusion* often means automatic action. *Defusion* lets you uncouple your behaviors from your internal experiences so that you can choose any behavior you want, especially those consistent with your values.

Use the Fusion Versus Defusion Worksheet (Worksheet 12-1), to keep track of examples of fusion and defusion this week.

Review of Acceptance

As discussed in previous sessions, there are many aspects of weight control that you do have control over. For example, you have control over the types of foods that are available in your home, planning meals and activity, and self-monitoring. You should use these strategies to facilitate healthy weight control behaviors as much as possible.

However, there are limits to what you can control about your weight loss experience. Some aspects of the obesogenic environment cannot be changed, and some ways in which the human mind and body work also are outside of your control. For example, you cannot control the number of fast-food restaurants or sidewalks that are in your neighborhood, or the hard-wired desire to eat palatable foods or stay resting on the couch. Together, biology and the environment can interact to make aspects of weight control challenging.

Some urges to eat palatable, high-calorie foods are inevitable. There is no magic pill that can make those go away. Acceptance of some of these challenging internal experiences is a key ingredient for willingness.

As discussed in Session 5 (refer back to pp. 37-42 for a review), acceptance is embracing your internal experiences—even those that may make it more challenging to engage in healthy behaviors—as part of being alive. It is not judging these internal experiences as good or bad, but instead being open to them. Most important, acceptance of internal experiences does not mean acceptance of behaviors that run counter to weight control. Instead, acceptance is the first step toward being willing to experience uncomfortable thoughts, feelings, urges, and other internal experiences and still choose to engage in a healthy behavior.

Urge Surfing

Using "control what you can" strategies often means that uncomfortable experiences happen less frequently. Some uncomfortable experiences are inevitable though. When they occur, one strategy that can help you become more willing to accept uncomfortable internal experiences is to practice "urge surfing." *Urge surfing* is the process by which you "ride the wave" of your thoughts, feelings, urges, or cravings, similar to how you would "ride" or "surf" a wave in the ocean.

By being mindful of your urges, you can surf them instead of sinking into them and acting on them. Rather than seeing the urge as "bad" and trying to get rid of or control the urge, you can accept the urge as the experience that you are having at that particular moment in time and allow yourself to experience the urge as it rises, crests, and falls. Surfing the urge does not mean acting on it! Instead, it involves "riding the urge out" until it eventually subsides.

Although urge surfing can be a very helpful tool for responding to urges, it is also important to use other skills you have learned to help reduce the likelihood of engaging in unhealthy behaviors when you experience strong urges or cravings. These strategies include keeping tempting foods out of your home, using portion control, and planning ahead.

Follow the "control what you can, accept what you can't" framework for urges. Control what you can by avoiding being in situations where you are likely to experience strong cravings or urges. When it is not possible to use these control-based strategies or when you experience strong urges or cravings despite implementing these other strategies, use urge surfing to accept and experience the urges without acting on them. Remember: You cannot control your internal experiences (thoughts, feelings, urges, cravings) and should practice accepting these. You can, however, control your behaviors. Practice accepting your internal experiences by urge surfing, while at the same time choosing to engage in healthy behaviors.

The following guidelines will help you to surf your urges instead of sinking into them and giving in:

1. *Acknowledge it.* Use the phrase "I am having the urge/thought/feeling . . ." to label the urge.
2. *Observe it.* Notice where you feel the urge in your body and what it feels like physically.
3. *Be open to it.* Rather than trying to suppress or get rid of the urge, practice accepting the experience of the urge. Try to refrain from labeling the urge as "bad" or "unacceptable."
4. *Watch the urge as it rises, crests, and then falls.* It may be helpful to score the intensity of the urge on a scale of 1 to 10 (1 = very low intensity, 10 = very high intensity) as you observe it. For example, you might say, "I'm having the urge to eat chips and the urge is now at a 7." Keep checking on the urge, noticing whether it is rising, peaking, or falling in intensity. Remember: No matter how huge the urge

gets, you have room for it. You can accept the urge—no matter how intense—as the experience you are having at that moment, and "ride" the wave until it eventually subsides.

This week, use the Urge Surfing Worksheet (Worksheet 12-2) to practice urge surfing using the guidelines outlined in this chapter.

Skill Builder for Session 12

Complete the following assignments before the next session:

☐ *Activity*: Exercise (e.g., brisk walking) for 30 minutes × 4 days (which is an increase from last session). Record type and minutes on your Keeping Track Form.

☐ *Behavior*: Work on the behavioral goal that you identified during today's session (specify goal here):

_____

_____

_____

☐ *Calories*: Follow a diet that is consistent with your calorie goal. Total the calories for each day (and for the week), calculate a seven-day average, and compare results to your calorie target.

☐ *Days Recorded*: Record every day.

☐ *Experiential Exercise*: (1) Complete the Fusion Versus Defusion Worksheet (Worksheet 12-1). (2) Complete the Urge Surfing Worksheet (Worksheet 12-2).

☐ *Reminder*: Complete your Check-In sheet before the next session. Also, don't forget to bring your Keeping Track Forms (or printout that includes foods, time eaten, and calories).

Instructions: Complete the items below *before* you attend Session 13.

A. *Activity*: Last week I exercised on _____ days, for an average of _____ minutes per day.

(The goal for last week was 4 × 30 minutes of activity.)

B. *Behavior*: The behavioral goal I set in session last week:

_____

_____

_____

I did/did not *(circle one)* achieve my behavioral goal.

C. *Calories*: My daily calorie goal was _____ and my daily calorie average was _____.

D. *Days Recorded*: I recorded my intake for _____ of the past seven days.

E. *Experiential Exercise*: I did/did not *(circle one)* complete the Fusion Versus Defusion Worksheet, and I did/did not *(circle one)* complete the Urge Surfing Worksheet.

CHAPTER 13

Session 13: Strategies to Help Defuse and Increase Willingness

Goals for This Session

- To review events of the past week and check in about progress
- To learn strategies to help defuse and increase willingness
- To discuss assignments for the coming week

Strategies to Help Defuse and Increase Willingness

There are several strategies that you can use to defuse from internal experiences, such as thoughts, feelings, and urges. These strategies can help you to step back from "sticky" internal experiences—that is, thoughts, feelings, and urges that make it difficult for you to engage in healthy behaviors. Stepping back from your internal experiences allows you to see them happening and to see them for what they really are: processes taking place in your brain or body. These strategies can also help you to uncouple your thoughts, feelings, and urges from your behaviors and increase willingness.

The following strategies can help you to defuse from "sticky" internal experiences and increase your willingness to engage in healthy behaviors:

1. *State the thought/feeling to yourself.* Use the phrase "I am having the thought that . . ." or "I am having the feeling that . . ." Labeling your internal experiences forces your mind to step back from the thought,

feeling, or urge, allowing you to gain a little space from it. This allows you to look *at* your thought/feeling rather than *from* it.

2. *Visualize your thoughts, feelings, and urges as leaves on a stream.* Visualize yourself looking down at a stream from a riverbank and picture each thought, feeling, or urge as a leaf on that stream. Watch your internal experiences float by on the stream.

3. *Replace the word "but" with the word "and"* when you have a thought about not being unable to engage in a healthy behavior because of a thought, feeling, or urge that you are experiencing. For example, when you have a thought such as "I was going to go for a walk, *but* I'm tired," replace the word "but" with the word "and" to get the following: "I was going to go for a walk, *and* I'm tired." Making this simple word substitution reminds you that your behaviors need not be dictated by your momentary thoughts and feelings and helps to uncouple your internal experiences (in this case, feeling tired) from your behaviors (going for a walk).

4. *"Thank" your mind or body* for the thought, feeling, and urge. Our minds are hard-wired to desire tasty foods, to want to avoid being physically active, and to provide reasons for why it is okay to eat certain foods and not be active. These tendencies helped our ancestors survive in times of food shortage. Although our food environment has changed and we no longer need to eat food whenever it is available or conserve energy to facilitate survival, our minds and bodies still produce these thoughts. Rather than being disappointed in yourself for having these thoughts, feelings, or urges, you can simply say, "thank you, mind" or "thank you, body" and recognize that your mind and body are just doing their jobs.

5. *"Just do it."* Have the thought, feeling, or urge and choose to engage in a behavior that runs *counter* to these thoughts, feelings, or urges anyway. Recognize that you can have thoughts, feelings, or urges that lead you to not want to engage in healthy behaviors, *and*, at the same time, you can make the healthy choice.

As with any new skill, you will need to practice using these defusion strategies to become effective at using them. It is very important that you set aside time each week to actively practice using these skills. Simply reading about defusion and thinking about how to use these skills is not enough! It is sort of like learning to play the piano. You can study how to play the piano and spend a lot of time thinking about what it would be like to put your fingers on the keys and play a song, but at some point you have to sit down and actually put your fingers on the keyboard if you want to learn how to play the piano. Although it may feel difficult to use these strategies at first, they will become easier to use the more you practice them.

This week, use the Practicing Defusion Worksheet (Worksheet 13-1) to practice using these strategies to defuse from powerful thoughts, feelings, and urges. Choose several situations in which you find yourself getting stuck to a thought, feeling, or urge, and use a defusion strategy to step back and get some distance from these internal experiences. For each strategy, record the thought, feeling, or urge that prompted the need for defusion. Then briefly discuss the behavioral outcome of using the strategy.

Skill Builder for Session 13

Complete the following assignments before the next session:

☐ *Activity*: Exercise (e.g., brisk walking) for 30 minutes × 4 days. Record type and minutes on your Keeping Track Form.

☐ *Behavior*: Work on the behavioral goal that you identified during today's session (specify goal here):

_____

_____

_____

☐ *Calories*: Follow a diet that is consistent with your calorie goal. Total the calories for each day (and for the week), calculate a seven-day average, and compare results to your calorie target.

☐ *Days Recorded*: Record every day.

☐ *Experiential Exercise*: Complete the Practicing Defusion Worksheet (Worksheet 13-1).

☐ *Reminder*: Complete your Check-In sheet before the next session. Also, don't forget to bring your Keeping Track Forms (or printout that includes foods, time eaten, and calories).

Instructions: Complete the items below *before* you attend Session 14.

A. *Activity*: Last week I exercised on _____ days, for an average of _____ minutes per day.

(The goal for last week was 4 × 30 minutes of activity.)

B. *Behavior*: The behavioral goal I set in session last week:

_____

_____

_____

I did/did not *(circle one)* achieve my behavioral goal.

C. *Calories*: My daily calorie goal was _____ and my daily calorie average was _____.

D. *Days Recorded*: I recorded my intake for _____ of the past seven days.

E. *Experiential Exercise*: I did/did not *(circle one)* complete the Practicing Defusion Worksheet.

CHAPTER 14

Session 14: Review of Dietary Principles, Mindless Eating (Part 1), and Portion Sizes

Goals for This Session

- To review events of the past week and check in about progress
- To review components of a healthy diet
- To learn about mindless eating
- To discuss portion sizes and how they impact weight control
- To discuss assignments for the coming week

Review of a Healthy Diet

There are several key components of a healthy and low-calorie diet. These include:

1. Fruits and vegetables
2. Lean protein
3. Whole grains

These types of foods facilitate weight control because they are filling without being extremely high in calories. Thus, you can eat a relatively large volume of these foods and feel full while consuming relatively few calories.

Although it is always important to track calories and be mindful of portion sizes, eating a high intake of these nutritious, low energy-dense foods will help you to feel satisfied while eating a diet that is nutritious and within your calorie goal.

See Session 2 (pp. 11–23) for a more detailed review of the components of a healthy diet, including information on reading nutrition labels for whole grains, specific examples of healthy foods to incorporate into your diet, and sample meal plans.

You can use the "control what you can, accept what you can't" philosophy as a framework for healthy eating. For example, you can continue to control what you can by:

- stocking your home with healthy, nutritious foods.
- eliminating tempting, high-calorie foods from your home.
- using portion control strategies to actively manage portion sizes.
- limiting how often you eat at restaurants.
- choosing behaviors that are consistent with your values and long-term goals.

You can also continue the practice of accepting what you cannot change by using willingness to choose the healthier option, even when it is not necessarily the most comfortable or pleasurable option. In addition, you can use urge surfing to facilitate eating a healthy diet. For example, you can surf the urge to stop at a fast-food restaurant for dinner instead of going home and eating a healthy meal as planned; you can surf the urge to eat donuts that are in the break room at work; and you surf the urge to buy tempting foods while grocery shopping to avoid purchasing and bringing these foods into the home.

Mindless Eating, Part 1

Mindless eating is eating that occurs without conscious intent, or even awareness.

Examples of mindless eating include:

- Eating while engaging in another behavior, such as cooking, watching television, or driving, and paying little or no attention to what you are eating or how much you are consuming.
- Eating in response to a negative thought, feeling, or bodily sensation (e.g., fatigue, urge) without carefully considering other options for responding to the internal experience or thinking about whether eating is an effective strategy for responding to this thought, feeling, or sensation.

■ Making a decision about eating (e.g., whether or not to eat, what to eat, or how much to eat) on "autopilot" without paying attention to this eating decision, the different eating behavior options in this situation, or the likely consequences of each option.

Portion Sizes

Portion sizes have increased a lot in the past several decades. Figure 14-1 gives examples of this kind of "portion distortion."

Figure 14-1

Examples of Portion Distortion

Table 14-1 Portion Control Strategies

Strategy	Example
Purchase single-serving versions of food.	Rather than buying a pint of ice cream to keep at home for a weekly dessert, buy just one single-serving of ice cream each week.
Transform unportioned food into portioned food.	Using plastic bags or small plastic containers, divide pretzels into 100-calorie portions for snacks throughout the week. Try doing this as soon as you get home; it will require less self-control that way.
Use smaller dishware.	Use the smaller version of a dinner plate and small serving utensils. It will be easier to take smaller portions of a meal when it still fills up the plate.
Serve yourself only how much you intend to eat.	After serving yourself dinner, put the rest away so that you aren't tempted to take a second helping just because you see the food there.

Because portion sizes have increased so much, it will be important for you to practice portion control strategies. See Table 14-1 for a list of portion control strategies and examples of how to implement them.

Skill Builder for Session 14

Complete the following assignments before the next session:

- ☐ *Activity*: Exercise (e.g., brisk walking) for 30 minutes × 4 days. Record type and minutes on your Keeping Track Form.
- ☐ *Behavior*: Choose and implement one portion control strategy.
- ☐ *Calories*: Follow a diet that is consistent with your calorie goal. Total the calories for each day (and for the week), calculate a seven-day average, and compare results to your calorie target.
- ☐ *Days Recorded*: Record every day.
- ☐ *Experiential Exercise*: N/A
- ☐ *Reminder*: Complete your Check-In sheet before the next session. Also, don't forget to bring your Keeping Track Forms (or printout that includes foods, time eaten, and calories).

Instructions: Complete the items below *before* you attend Session 15.

A. *Activity*: Last week I exercised on _____ days, for an average of _____ minutes per day.

(The goal for last week was 4 × 30 minutes of activity.)

B. *Behavior*: I did/did not *(circle one)* choose and implement one portion control strategy.

C. *Calories*: My daily calorie goal was _____ and my daily calorie average was _____.

D. *Days Recorded*: I recorded my intake for _____ of the past seven days.

E. *Experiential Exercise*: N/A

CHAPTER 15

Session 15: Mindless Eating (Part 2) and Mindful Decision-Making

Goals for This Session

- To review events of the past week and check in about progress
- To identify the dangers associated with mindless eating
- To learn strategies for maximizing mindful decision-making
- To discuss assignments for the coming week

Mindless Eating, Part 2

Dangers of Mindless Eating

Session 14 provided examples of situations in which people tend to eat mindlessly. Mindless eating is problematic for long-term weight control. There are two primary dangers associated with mindless eating:

1. *Lack of monitoring.* Because you are not paying conscious attention to your eating behavior when engaging in mindless eating, you are not monitoring the amount of food that you are eating. As a result, you may consume more calories than intended. It also can be difficult to accurately record calories consumed.

2. *Lack of conscious decision-making awareness.* Because you are not paying deliberate attention to the decisions you are making when engaged in mindless eating, you may make eating choices that you will regret.

In particular, you may be more likely to make eating choices that prioritize short-term (and short-lived) rewards over long-term rewards.

Mindful Decision-Making

Mindful decision-making is a skill that you can use to prevent mindless eating and mindless decision-making. *Mindful decision-making* involves increasing your awareness, attention, and intention when making decisions about what and how much to eat. This skill requires practice and intention, but can be very helpful for preventing mindless eating.

There are three strategies that can be practiced to increase mindful decision-making:

1. *"Stop, think."* Stop and think before you eat! Oftentimes, decisions about eating happen so quickly and occur so automatically that it can feel as though there was no decision point at all. Just as you "think before you speak," practice thinking before you eat. Take a moment to make a deliberate decision about *whether* to eat, *what* to eat, and *how much* to eat. Practice calling to mind the phrase "Stop, think" when in situations where there is food present to remind yourself to pause and think before eating.

2. *Slow down and pay deliberate attention to the decision-making process.* Take the time to notice the external cues (sights, sounds, smells) that make you want to eat. Slow down and note the internal cues (thoughts, urges, feelings) that are pushing you to eat. Pay extra attention to these cues in situations where eating has become a habit. Imagine yourself as a sports commentator who is reporting on every aspect of your decision-making process.

3. *Make every decision a deliberate up or down vote on a value (or something you care about).* As discussed in Sessions 7 and 10 (for a review, see pp. 49–52 and pp. 65–68), values are the ideas, principles, and domains in our lives that are most precious to us. When making decisions about eating, ask yourself if each decision is a vote up or a vote down on your values. Imagining that your decisions are votes for or against what you care most about can help you consider the long-term consequences of your decisions in the moments you are making them. This technique can combat the tendency to make mindless decisions that prioritize short-term (and short-lived) rewards over long-term rewards.

These mindful decision-making strategies can also be used to maximize mindful decision-making related to other behaviors, such as physical activity. For example, you can use the "up or down vote on a value" strategy when deciding whether to go for a walk as planned or skip the walk.

This week, use the Mindful Decision-Making Worksheet (Worksheet 15-1) to practice mindful decision-making with regard to food and physical activity. On each of the next seven days, choose an eating or activity decision point to practice making mindful eating and activity choices. It can be especially helpful to identify instances in which you might eat mindlessly (such as munching on popcorn in a movie theater) or make mindless decisions about eating or activity. Use the strategies discussed in group to be especially mindful during the situation. For each day, record the situation, the strategy (stop and think, values vote, slowing, or other) and the outcome.

Skill Builder for Session 15

Complete the following assignments before the next session:

- ☐ *Activity*: Exercise (e.g., brisk walking) for 30 minutes × 4 days. Record type and minutes on your Keeping Track Form.

- ☐ *Behavior*: Choose a specific strategy to improve the accuracy of your Keeping Track Form (e.g., always record right after eating, keep your form in a visible location, weigh/measure all foods, record planned food in advance).

- ☐ *Calories*: Follow a diet that is consistent with your calorie goal. Total the calories for each day (and for the week), calculate a seven-day average, and compare results to your calorie target.

- ☐ *Days Recorded*: Record every day.

- ☐ *Experiential Exercise*: Use the Mindful Decision-Making Worksheet (Worksheet 15-1) to practice mindful decision-making with regard to food or physical activity. Each day for the next seven days, choose an eating/activity decision point and use the strategies discussed in the session. For each day, record (1) the situation, (2) the strategy utilized, and (3) the outcome.

- ☐ *Reminder*: Complete your Check-In sheet before the next session. Also, don't forget to bring your Keeping Track Forms (or printout that includes foods, time eaten, and calories).

Instructions: Complete the items below *before* you attend Session 16.

A. *Activity*: Last week I exercised on _____ days, for an average of _____ minutes per day.

(The goal for last week was 4 × 30 minutes of activity.)

B. *Behavior*: I did/did not *(circle one)* choose a specific strategy to improve the accuracy of my Keeping Track Form.

C. *Calories*: My daily calorie goal was _____ and my daily calorie average was _____.

D. *Days Recorded*: I recorded my intake for _____ of the past seven days.

E. *Experiential Exercise*: I did/did not *(circle one)* complete the Mindful Decision-Making Worksheet.

CHAPTER 16 | Session 16: Transitioning to Biweekly Meetings

Goals for This Session

- To review events of the past week and check in about progress
- To plan for the transition to biweekly meetings
- To review skills learned thus far in the program
- To learn how to conduct a Weekly Review on your own
- To discuss assignments for the coming weeks

Transitioning to Biweekly Meetings

Congratulations on completing the first phase of the program! The time and energy you have spent attending sessions and setting and achieving behavioral goals thus far demonstrates your commitment to yourself and your health values. You have made many important changes that will be crucial to your long-term success. From now on, sessions will gradually become less frequent. This will allow you to spend more time practicing the skills that you have mastered so far, while also gradually coming to depend on *yourself* to maintain these changes long term.

The next several sessions will focus on building skills for *keeping the weight off in the long term*. You will learn how to deal with lapses, monitor your weight, and evaluate your behavior after the program ends. During this time, the work you do on your own outside of sessions becomes even more important. The more you practice skills between sessions, the better prepared you will be to maintain these changes over the long term.

Session attendance continues to be vital to your progress. From now on, an absence from even one session could mean missing out on a month or more of support and interrupts the gradual step-down in frequency that has been carefully built into the program. This is a good opportunity to recommit yourself to the program and to prioritize consistent attendance for the remainder of the program.

Overall Skill Review

This program differs from many other weight loss programs in that it is focused on maintaining weight losses over the long term and viewing the behavioral changes you are making as lifestyle modifications, rather than short-term strategies to use only while actively losing weight.

You have worked hard to accomplish important changes to your eating patterns and physical activity, incorporating strategies such as self-monitoring, engineering your home food environment, planning meals, and scheduling activity into your daily routine. You have also learned how psychological strategies (e.g., willingness, mindful decision-making, defusion, and focusing on values) can help you continue enacting these key weight control behaviors in the long term. Using the Skill Review Worksheet (Worksheet 16-1) as a guide, think about which strategies will be key for you moving forward and in which situations each will be most helpful.

Completing Weekly Reviews at Home

As session frequency decreases, you will have the opportunity to practice gaining more personal accountability. Just like monitoring daily food intake or activity, monitoring your overall weight control progress is a skill that is built over time. You will practice it each week that you do not have a program session by completing a Weekly Review as shown in Appendix D. Being aware of weekly changes in exercise patterns, self-monitoring, and weight will allow you to act quickly to prevent significant weight regain.

The following are tips for completing Weekly Reviews at home:

- *Commit to a specific day and time* during which you can complete your Weekly Review *each week.* Different days of the week work better for different people, but make sure that the time you select is one that you can do on a consistent basis (e.g., Saturday mornings, when you are typically at home in the morning, have access to a digital scale, and have time to sit down and reflect on the past week).

- Many find it helpful to set a reminder (e.g., in a calendar, on a smartphone) for the scheduled day and time.

- *Weigh yourself on a regular basis.* It is recommended that you weigh yourself *once per week at a minimum*, but many people find that daily weighing is more helpful to stay on track.

  - On the morning of your Weekly Review, weigh yourself right away, before you eat or drink anything and after you have used the bathroom.
  - Note: If you prefer to complete the Weekly Review in the evening, it is still important to weigh yourself in the morning. This will provide the most consistent and accurate weight possible.

- *Keep a weekly record/chart* of your weight changes over time. You may be able to remember your weight from last week, but it will be difficult to remember several weeks' worth of weights without having a record of them. Keeping a weight graph (or weight chart) allows you to observe changes over time, and it provides you with objective information about whether your behavior is translating into weight loss. Eventually (after this program ends), you will be relying solely on these weekly check-ins to monitor and maintain your weight losses over the long term. You can use Appendix C: Home Weight Change Record to track your weight on a graph or a table (or both), whichever method you find most helpful.

- *Allow yourself sufficient time*, in a quiet environment, so that you will be able to complete all components of the Weekly Review. Be sure to take time to consider the following:

  - What were your goals (including weight loss, behavioral, calorie, and physical activity) for the past week? Were you able to achieve them?
  - If not, what got in the way? What will you do differently next week?
  - If so, what helped you do so? How will you continue this moving forward?

Complete the following assignments before the next session:

☐ *Activity*: Exercise (e.g., brisk walking) for 30 minutes × 5 days (which is an increase from last session). Record type and minutes on your Keeping Track Form.

☐ *Behavior*: Purchase a digital scale to weigh yourself regularly, if one is not readily available.

Complete your Weekly Review sheet (Appendix D) in the off-week(s) between now and the next session.

☐ *Calories*: Follow a diet that is consistent with your calorie goal. Total the calories for each day (and for the week), calculate a seven-day average, and compare results to your calorie target.

☐ *Days Recorded*: Record every day.

☐ *Experiential Exercise*: Complete the Skill Review Worksheet (Worksheet 16-1).

☐ *Reminder*: Complete your Check-In sheet before the next session. Also, don't forget to bring your Keeping Track Forms (or printout that includes foods, time eaten, and calories) and Home Weight Change Record.

Instructions: Complete the items below *before* you attend Session 17.

A. *Activity*:

Week 1: I exercised on _____ days, for an average of _____ minutes per day.

Week 2: I exercised on _____ days, for an average of _____ minutes per day.

(The goal for last week was 5 × 30 minutes of activity for each week.)

B. *Behavior*:

I did/did not *(circle one)* purchase a scale last week *or* I already have a scale at home.

I did/did not *(circle one)* complete the Weekly Review at home.

C. *Calories*:

My daily calorie goal was _____ and my daily calorie average was

Week 1: _____ calories.

Week 2: _____ calories.

D. *Days Recorded*: I recorded my intake for _____ of the past 14 days.

E. *Experiential Exercise*: I did/did not *(circle one)* complete the Skill Review Worksheet.

CHAPTER 17

Session 17: Maintaining Losses Over the Long Term

Goals for This Session

- To review events of the past weeks and check in about progress
- To learn about the keys behaviors for successful long-term weight loss maintenance
- To make a plan for your own success
- To discuss assignments for the coming weeks

How Do People Succeed at Weight Loss?

For many people seeking treatment for weight loss, this is not their first attempt at losing the weight and keeping it off. In fact, it's most common for clients to report having lost weight many times in the past, only to regain the weight (or more) afterward. If this describes you, you are certainly not alone. As you've already learned in this program, controlling weight is difficult for anyone—due to our obesogenic food environment and our human "wiring" that leads us to seek pleasure from high-calorie foods and a sedentary lifestyle.

The good news is that many people are successful at keeping the weight off for the long term, despite these challenges. Some of these people are members of a special club, called the National Weight Control Registry (NWCR). These members have met very specific requirements in order to join the registry: they must have lost 30 pounds or more and kept it off for at least a year. On average, these individuals have actually lost about 70 pounds and kept it off for almost six years! So who are these NWCR members, and what helps make them so successful at maintaining their weight losses for the long term? This session will provide you with a peek into the lives of these successful weight-loss maintainers.

Who Are the Members of the National Weight Control Registry?

Members are quite diverse in the amount of weight they have lost (anywhere from 30 to 300 pounds) and how quickly they lost the weight in the first place (over a period of several months to up to 14 years). The key thing to remember is that these successful weight maintainers are everyday people—just like you—who have found ways to engage in key behaviors that ensure their long-term success. Take a look at Box 17-1 to learn some key characteristics of these members.

What Are the Key Differences Between Successful and Unsuccessful Weight Loss Attempts?

When registry members report on their weight control approaches and identify what was different about *this successful weight loss attempt*, two themes consistently emerge:

1. Registry members report that, this time, they were *more committed* to behavior change and weight loss. They made weight maintenance a *top priority* and *stayed focused* on their ultimate goal of weight control.

Box 17-1 Becoming a Weight Maintenance Pro: A Snapshot of the NWCR

Who are the NWCR Members?

- Over 4,000 members
- Mostly women
- On average, members are in their mid-40s, but the registry has members of all ages
- Long-time struggles with weight: many report being overweight as a child and having one or two parents who were overweight
- Many report a triggering event that motivated their weight loss (e.g., developing diabetes, relative having a heart attack)

---

2. Members also say that they *dieted more strictly* and engaged in more *physical activity* than they did in previous attempts. *Over 90% of registry members say they used both diet and exercise to lose weight and maintain it.*

How Do They Maintain Their Weight Loss?

To help us understand what key behaviors promote long-term weight loss success, members of the registry are asked to fill out questionnaires about their eating habits and physical activity. Reviewing their answers suggests that there are certain typical approaches to successful weight loss maintenance:

1. Successful weight losers report eating a low-calorie, low-fat diet. On average, these members report eating about *1,400 calories per day* (which translates to 1,800 calories with error of estimation included). They also report getting no more than 24–27% of their daily calories from fat. This is far below the average American, who eats closer to 36% of calories from fat.

2. Very few members eat a low-carbohydrate diet (like Atkins or South Beach). Rather, these individuals *report eating a high-carbohydrate, low-fat diet*, with a wide variety of fresh fruits, vegetables, and low-fat whole-grain products.

3. Most NWCR members (78%) report eating *breakfast* every day. Only 4% report that they never eat breakfast. The breakfast typically includes cereal, fruit, and milk. NWCR members who report eating breakfast have an overall daily caloric intake that is no higher than people who skipped breakfast.

4. NWCR members report five eating episodes per day (*breakfast, lunch, dinner, and two snacks*). They report eating out about three times per week, but go to fast-food restaurants less than once per week.

5. Physical activity is a major factor in their weight loss maintenance success. Registry members engage in about *an hour a day of physical activity, most days of the week.* Walking was the most frequently cited physical activity, but aerobic dance, cycling, and strength training are also reported frequently. The amount of physical activity reported by NWCR members far exceeds the Surgeon General's recommendation to exercise for 30 minutes on most days of the week.

6. Registry members *weigh themselves* regularly. Almost half of the members weigh themselves every day, and three-quarters weigh themselves at least once a week.

7. Registry members were asked whether they watched their diet and physical activity as closely on weekends as they do during the week (or as closely on vacations/holidays as they do during the rest of the year). About half reported that they were equally careful at both times and the other half said they were more careful on weekdays or normal/routine days (i.e., days that were not holidays, birthdays, or vacation days). Researchers followed these two groups for over a year to see which group did better. The researchers found that those *individuals who were equally careful on both weekdays and weekends (and on holidays and routine days) were less likely to regain weight* over the year of follow-up. Why might this be true? Perhaps members who give themselves "breaks" from diet and exercise on weekends also start giving themselves "breaks" at other times, and thus end up eating more and exercising less over time.

Create Your Plan for Long-Term Weight Loss Maintenance Success

Do you have to follow the exact same plan as NWCR participants to become a successful maintainer? The answer is no. In fact, among Registry participants, there is no "one plan fits all" approach. As evidenced by the members' stories, there is a great deal of variability in what individuals do to become successful maintainers. Each person has found a way that worked for him or her—an approach that could be sustained long term. For example, some people are best able to sustain a low-calorie diet using an Atkins-like low-carbohydrate approach. *The key is to find an approach that works for you and start to own your weight loss success*!

Now that you've learned about the NWCR, take some time to reflect on how your current behaviors "measure up" to those of successful weight loss maintainers. Using the How Do You Compare to the NWCR Members? Worksheet (Worksheet 17-1) as a guide, think about what you are currently already doing that is in line with NWCR members' strategies. Chances are, you're already enacting many of the behaviors that are so key to long-term success. This is a good time to think about which strategies you might want to add in moving forward. On the Your Weight Maintenance Plan for Success Worksheet (Worksheet 17-2), start developing your long-term weight loss maintenance plan, which should include the behaviors you have already mastered, as well as behaviors you can still improve on.

We know that many of the behaviors necessary for weight control are difficult to keep up over the long term. The psychological strategies you have learned about in this program are particularly helpful for maintaining these weight control behaviors. For example, self-monitoring over the long term can be facilitated by increased willingness, as well as keeping your values in the forefront of your mind. Using the Using Psychological Strategies to Maintain Weight Control Behaviors Worksheet (Worksheet 17-3) as a guide, spend time thinking about which psychological strategies you will use to continue engaging in each of your chosen weight control behaviors, *even when* you hit a bump in the road on your weight control journey or your motivation fluctuates.

Remember that although long-term weight control requires commitment to maintaining new behaviors for a lifetime, many people have achieved success. Spend some time browsing the NWCR website at www.nwcr.ws. Members' success stories are listed on the site, along with information about how you can become a member in the future.

Skill Builder for Session 17

Complete the following assignments before the next session:

☐ *Activity*: Exercise (e.g., brisk walking) for 30 minutes × 5 days. Record type and minutes on your Keeping Track Form.

☐ *Behavior*: Follow the goals identified on the Your Weight Maintenance Plan for Success Worksheet (Worksheet 17-2).

Complete your Weekly Review sheet (Appendix D) in the off-week(s) between now and the next session.

☐ *Calories*: Follow a diet that is consistent with your calorie goal. Total the calories for each day (and for the week), calculate a seven-day average, and compare results to your calorie target.

☐ *Days Recorded*: Record every day.

☐ *Experiential Exercise*: Complete the Using Psychological Strategies to Maintain Weight Control Behaviors Worksheet (Worksheet 17-3).

☐ *Reminder*: Complete your Check-In sheet before the next session. Also, don't forget to bring your Keeping Track Forms (or printout that includes foods, time eaten, and calories) and Home Weight Change Record.

Instructions: Complete the items below *before* you attend Session 18.

A. *Activity*:

   Week 1: I exercised on _____ days, for an average of _____ minutes per day.

   Week 2: I exercised on _____ days, for an average of _____ minutes per day.

   (The goal for last week was 5 × 30 minutes of activity for each week.)

B. *Behavior*:

   I did/did not *(circle one)* follow the goals identified on the Your Weight Maintenance Plan for Success Worksheet.

   I did/did not *(circle one)* complete the Weekly Review at home last week.

C. *Calories*:

   My daily calorie goal was _____ and my daily calorie average was:

   Week 1: _____ calories.

   Week 2: _____ calories.

D. *Days Recorded* I recorded my intake for _____ of the past 14 days.

E. *Experiential Exercise*:

   I did/did not *(circle one)* complete the Using Psychological Strategies to Maintain Weight Control Behaviors Worksheet.

CHAPTER 18

Session 18: Willingness and Reducing Barriers to Physical Activity

Goals for This Session

- To review events of the past weeks and check in about progress
- To review the concept of willingness
- To create a plan to overcome barriers to physical activity
- To discuss assignments for the coming weeks

Willingness: Learning to Drive With Your "Passengers on the Bus"

Willingness is the skill of engaging in valued behavior no matter what the effect on your thoughts/feelings. When it comes to physical activity, your mind can give you plenty of reasons to seek comfort and be sedentary, rather than to exercise. Your mind might tell you that you don't have time to exercise, that it's too cold or rainy outside to exercise, or that you're too tired. Practicing willingness can help you engage in physical activity regardless of your thoughts and feelings.

In many ways, living a valued life is like driving a bus on the highway toward your values. Each mile you drive takes you that much closer toward your values, but the highway never ends. (Remember—you can always take further action to move toward your values. They are a direction in life, not a destination.) As drivers on the highway of life, we all take some "passengers" along with us for the ride. These passengers are the internal experiences we carry with us on a daily basis—our thoughts, feelings, and physical sensations. Unfortunately, some of these passengers can be noisy or annoying, and they might not always quiet down when we want them to. For example, the passenger that tells you it would be much more comfortable to hit the snooze button and sleep in, rather than go out for a morning walk, might nag at you every morning. Oftentimes, you may find that these passengers encourage you to take action that moves you away from, not closer to, your values.

Willingness can help you continue moving toward your values and avoid getting side-tracked or slowed down by these passengers. Possible strategies include:

- Keeping values in mind
- Accepting that these thoughts will inevitably arise
- Being willing to have these thoughts, while still driving toward your valued direction

Applying Willingness to Physical Activity

Take time to reflect back over the past several months of this program and think about your biggest barriers to being physically active. Also consider the most effective strategies you have used (or would like to try using more often) that will help you overcome these barriers.

- What are some instances in which you have used willingness to engage in physical activity, even when your passengers were trying to side-track you?
- What are the most common passengers (thoughts/feelings/ sensations) that get in the way of your physical activity?
- Can you remember times in the past when you have listened to these passengers? What was the result?
- Which strategies have been the most helpful for you to overcome these barriers and be active, *no matter* what your mind is telling you?

Although we cannot control our thoughts, feelings, and physical sensations, we can control our behavior in response to these experiences. Successful long-term weight control requires a commitment to choosing behaviors that are in line with your values, regardless of those experiences.

Complete the following assignments before the next session:

☐ *Activity*: Exercise (e.g., brisk walking) for 40 minutes × 5 days (which is an increase from last session). Record type and minutes on your Keeping Track Form.

☐ *Behavior*: Complete your Weekly Review sheet (Appendix D) in the off-week(s) between now and the next session.

Work on the behavioral goal that you identified during today's session (specify goal here):

_____

_____

_____

☐ *Calories*: Follow a diet that is consistent with your calorie goal. Total the calories for each day (and for the week), calculate a seven-day average, and compare results to your calorie target.

☐ *Days Recorded*: Record every day.

☐ *Experiential Exercise*: Complete the Overcoming Barriers to Physical Activity Worksheet (Worksheet 18-1).

☐ *Reminder*: Complete your Check-In sheet before the next session. Also, don't forget to bring your Keeping Track Forms (or printout that includes foods, time eaten, and calories) and Home Weight Change Record.

Instructions: Complete the items below *before* you attend Session 19.

A. *Activity*:

Week 1: I exercised on _____ days, for an average of _____ minutes per day.

Week 2: I exercised on _____ days, for an average of _____ minutes per day.

(The goal for last week was 5 × 40 minutes of activity for each week.)

B. *Behavior*:

I did/did not *(circle one)* complete the Weekly Review at home last week.

The behavioral goal I set in session last week:

_____

_____

_____

I did/did not *(circle one)* achieve my behavioral goal.

C. *Calories*:

My daily calorie goal was _____ and my daily calorie average was

Week 1: _____ calories.

Week 2: _____ calories.

D. *Days Recorded:*

I recorded my intake for _____ of the past 14 days.

E. *Experiential Exercise*

I did/did not *(circle one)* complete the Overcoming Barriers to Physical Activity Worksheet.

Goals for This Session

- To review events of the past weeks and check in about progress
- To introduce a new concept called committed action
- To review the strategies for committed action
- To publically commit to a long-term goal related to weight control
- To discuss assignments for the coming weeks

Introduction to Committed Action

The reality of long-term weight control is that, even with all of the skills you have learned from this program, there are still challenges to maintaining your new healthy lifestyle. Take a moment to think of some challenges that you may face (or have already encountered) while maintaining the behaviors you have learned thus far in the program.

Challenges to long-term weight control:

_____

_____

_____

_____

You might notice two themes in your responses. One substantial challenge to long-term weight control is that motivation often declines over time. *Maintaining* weight loss may begin to feel less "rewarding" than actively *losing* weight. When you become less motivated, it is typically easy to lose sight of values (e.g., longevity, health) that can make maintaining a healthy lifestyle more rewarding. A second challenge is that the factors that influence eating and exercise behaviors (e.g., social support, stress, cravings, emotions) tend to ebb and flow over time. This means that it may not always feel like the conditions are "ideal" for continuing to stay committed to weight control. For example, if your hours change at work and you can no longer go to the gym at your normal time, you might be tempted to stop exercising. Another good example is experiencing a craving for French fries completely out of the blue, when you have not eaten French fries for months. Will you be able to stay committed to your values of weight control, even when these conditions have changed?

This session is focused on a skill called *committed action*, which is *the act of maintaining a behavior consistent with your values regardless of how easy or hard it is.* Given that you have been in the program for some time now, it is likely that you are already engaging in committed action. For example, engaging in committed action means that you go for your morning walk each day regardless of changes in the weather. Take a moment to write down examples of how you are already engaging in committed action. Examples of committed action:

_____

_____

_____

_____

Think of committed action as hiking up a mountain. Hiking up a mountain can involve hard work, and there will be times when there are trees or foggy weather that block your view. When these obstacles get in your way, you may not be certain that you are even moving in the right direction. However, if someone else was across the valley and looking at you through binoculars, she could see that you are going precisely in the right direction. Committed action is staying the course even when you cannot easily see the progress that you are making. Just like the hiker, you will experience challenges related to maintaining a healthy lifestyle. Remember that *success is measured by continuing to move forward regardless of imperfect conditions.*

Table 19-1 Strategies for Committed Action

Remember you are response-able	You are *able* to respond to the situations in which it might be difficult to maintain healthy lifestyle changes. *You* have the power to choose how to behave.
Use language that reminds you of your response-ability	Try to begin phrases with "I am the person who . . ." Example: "I am the person who decided to lose weight. I am the person who stuck with my calorie goal for the past 11 days. I am the person who has been keeping track of my calorie intake since I started this program."
Keep your goals visible	Write your goals down on note-cards, or anywhere else where you can keep them visible. Be sure to periodically switch the location so the reminder stays prominent.
Share your goals and values	Share your goals and values with people who you care about. This will create accountability to someone other than yourself.

Strategies for Committed Action

There are many ways in which you can engage in committed action. See Table 19-1 for a list of suggestions.

Stand and Commit

Another way that you can stay committed to the healthy behaviors that you care about is to publically announce your intentions to commit. This session will focus on building the skills to choose a commitment, publically state that commitment, and use committed action strategies outlined in Table 19-1 to keep that commitment. Follow these guidelines for choosing a commitment for this exercise:

1. Think of a behavior that is *key to weight control success* and that also requires *mindfulness* and *commitment*.
2. *Be specific* about the commitment, and include exact details of your plan.
3. Choose a commitment that is *challenging*, but that you are fairly confident you can honor.

Record your commitment here:

_____

_____

You will complete the Committed Action Worksheet (Worksheet 19-1) as part of your Skill Builder over the next few weeks, where you will record your commitments, as well as anticipated challenges and helpful strategies that will help you stay committed. Next session, you will check in regarding whether or not you were able to stay committed and what skills you used to do so.

Skill Builder for Session 19

Complete the following assignments before the next session:

☐ *Activity*: Exercise (e.g., brisk walking) for 40 minutes × 5 days. Record type and minutes on your Keeping Track Form.

☐ *Behavior*: Carry out the behavior you committed to during the "Stand and Commit" activity (which you recorded earlier).

Complete your Weekly Review sheet (Appendix D) in the off-week(s) between now and the next session.

☐ *Calories*: Follow a diet that is consistent with your calorie goal. Total the calories for each day (and for the week), calculate a seven-day average, and compare results to your calorie target.

☐ *Days Recorded*: Record every day.

☐ *Experiential Exercise*: Complete the Committed Action Worksheet (Worksheet 19-1).

☐ *Reminder*: Complete your Check-In sheet before the next session. Also, don't forget to bring your Keeping Track Forms (or printout that includes foods, time eaten, and calories) and Home Weight Change Record.

Instructions: Complete the items below *before* you attend Session 20.

A. *Activity*:

   Week 1: I exercised on _____ days, for an average of _____ minutes per day.

   Week 2: I exercised on _____ days, for an average of _____ minutes per day.

   (The goal for last week was 5 × 40 minutes of activity.)

B. *Behavior*:

   I did/did not *(circle one)* carry out the behavior I committed to during the "Stand and Commit" activity (which you recorded earlier).

   I did/did not *(circle one)* complete the Weekly Review at home last week.

C. *Calories*:

   My daily calorie goal was _____ and my daily calorie average was

   Week 1: _____ calories

   Week 2: _____ calories

D. *Days Recorded*:

   I recorded my intake for _____ of the past 14 days.

E. *Experiential Exercise*:

   I did/did not *(circle one)* complete the Committed Action Worksheet.

CHAPTER 20

Session 20: Overeating and Emotional Eating

Goals for This Session

- To review events of the past weeks and check in about progress
- To discuss overeating episodes and how to prevent them
- To discuss emotional eating and alternative responses to emotions
- To discuss assignments for the coming weeks

Preventing Overeating Episodes

Overeating episodes are characterized by eating more in one sitting than you intended to. Preventing these overeating episodes is critical for long-term weight control. Take a moment to consider what strategies you have used to prevent overeating.

Strategies to prevent overeating:

_____

_____

_____

_____

Some of the most effective strategies to prevent overeating are "control what you can" methods. This means that there are ways in which you can change your behavior or your environment to make it less likely that you

Table 20-1 Coping With Overeating Episodes

Strategy	Description
Engineer your environment	Control availability of certain foods in the environment to make it much less likely that those foods will ultimately be overeaten.
Control portion sizes	To limit intake: ▪ Avoid eating directly from a large container (e.g., full-sized bag of chips or cookies) or family-style (i.e., dishes of food placed on the dining room table). ▪ Preportion foods immediately upon purchase and place anticipated leftovers in the fridge or freezer before eating a meal. These strategies create barriers that prompt you to make a more conscious decision about whether to have more.
Follow a regular schedule of eating	Avoid becoming so intensely hungry that having control of your eating becomes more difficult.
Identify triggers of overeating	Understand more about what puts you at high risk for overeating and then target those risk factors.

will engage in overeating behavior. See Table 20-1 for a list of strategies that you might try to prevent overeating.

Identifying triggers for overeating is an especially important strategy. Identifying the specific situations, times, events, and emotions that typically trigger overeating will give you more information about how to intervene to prevent overeating. For example, if you notice that you typically overeat in the evening while watching TV, then you might choose to intervene by doing something else with your time in the evening or using portion control to be more mindful of your consumption while watching TV. Complete the Identifying Triggers of Overeating Worksheet (Worksheet 20-1) to "take inventory" of your specific overeating triggers.

Emotional Eating

One trigger for overeating can be emotions (e.g., when you feel sad, happy, angry, bored). When we use eating as a way to cope with emotions, we call this *emotional eating*. Take a moment to consider if you have ever had an experience of eating in response to an emotion.

Example of eating in response to emotions:

_____

_____

_____

_____

It is common for people to form a habit of emotional eating. This habit works much like a cycle. If eating has temporarily reduced emotional discomfort in the past, the brain recognizes this to be rewarding. The next time you feel that same emotional discomfort, the brain is likely to remember that delicious food has previously "resolved" this issue and becomes hardwired to seek out food in response to those emotional experiences. See Figure 20-1 for an illustration of the emotional eating cycle.

This cycle is at work in your everyday life, when you experience a strong (seemingly unconscious) desire to eat whenever you experience an uncomfortable emotion. Consider how effective emotional eating is as a way of coping with sadness, anger, stress, boredom, happiness, or other types of emotions.

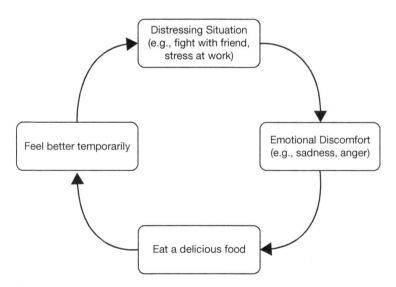

Figure 20-1

Cycle of Emotional Eating

Does eating provide you with relief from emotions?

_____

_____

_____

_____

How long does this relief last?

_____

_____

_____

_____

How do you feel about yourself after an emotional eating episode? How do you feel about your weight control?

_____

_____

_____

_____

People often find that the relief experienced by eating is short-lived (sometimes only lasting for mere seconds). However, there are long-term costs to emotional eating, such as feeling guilty or frustrated and experiencing small weight gains (from excess calorie intake). It can be a frustrating experience if you have engaged in this habit for a long time, and it may feel as if the cycle is unbreakable.

The good news is that because emotional eating is a habit that you have learned over time, you can also _unlearn_ it! There are steps that you can take (see Table 20-2) to break the habit of emotional eating and _replace it with new ways of responding to your emotions._

Establishing healthy responses is a _key step_ in breaking the pattern of eating in response to emotions. It is important to _replace eating_ with a different response that is more consistent with your values (e.g., health, long-term weight control). This can be done through choosing a deliberate (or alternative) response. Use the suggestions in Table 20-3 to choose a

Table 20-2 Establishing New Patterns of Responding to Emotions

Strategy	Description
Build awareness	Notice when emotions rise and name them. Also identify the idea that seems to be causing them. Here are some common sources of emotion. ▪ Expecting harm → Anxiety ▪ Experiencing loss → Sadness ▪ Deciding rights were violated → Anger ▪ Believing you've disgraced yourself → Embarrassment Use Rate Your Emotional Eating (Worksheet 20-2) to gain a better awareness of which specific emotions lead to urges to eat for you personally.
Notice your response to your emotions	▪ Are you judging your emotions or treating them as simply existing? ▪ Are you pushing them away or accepting them? ▪ Notice any urges to eat. ▪ Practice adopting an accepting attitude: Don't judge your emotions or try to get them to go away.
Uncouple emotion and action	▪ Refrain from eating. ▪ Impulses to eat in response to emotions do not mean that your action needs to follow suit. ▪ It is possible for you to feel a difficult emotion and to still adhere to a healthy diet.
Establish healthy responses	▪ Choose a deliberate action that you consider a healthy response. ▪ Actively work to make the situation better. ▪ Engage in a fulfilling activity.

deliberate action in response to emotions *instead* of eating. For homework, record these deliberate actions on the Healthy Behaviors I Will Choose in Response to Difficult Emotions Worksheet (Worksheet 20-3).

It is important to remember that emotions are internal experiences that we cannot control. With this exercise, we are employing the "control what you can, accept what you can't" program philosophy. Choosing a deliberate action (rather than eating) in response to an emotion is a "control what you can" strategy. You can control your behavior. However, you cannot control how you feel. Thus, if you are feeling upset or angry, consider this an "accept what you can't" control experience and apply the psychological strategies you have learned throughout the program.

You may find that these alternative activities result in emotions becoming less intense, or you may find that they feel just the same. Use this as an opportunity to practice *flexibility* by choosing the deliberate action no matter how much you would like to engage in a habitual response (eating).

Table 20-3 Deliberate Actions in Response to Emotions

Activating Activities	Soothing Activities
Walking	Lighting a candle
Jogging	Looking at beautiful art/scenery
Exercise class	Watching the stars
Cleaning	Going to a beautiful place
Washing dishes	Listening to or playing soothing music
Vacuuming	Enjoying nature
Dusting	Singing
Gardening	Meditating
Calling a friend/family member	Smelling favorite perfume
Shopping	Using favorite lotion
Watching a favorite movie	Enjoying smells of nature or flowers
Reading a favorite book	Taking a bubble bath
Watching a favorite TV show	Taking a shower
Listening to a podcast	Getting a massage
Reading a magazine	Spending time with pet
Reading a newspaper	Soaking feet
Playing a game	Brushing hair
Working on a puzzle	Doing nails
Volunteering	Imagining relaxing scene/safe place
Giving someone a present	Imagining distress floating away
Doing something thoughtful	Focusing on positive aspects of life
Making something for someone	Praying
Writing in a journal	Listening to relaxation tape
Drawing/painting/sculpting	Tensing and releasing muscles
Listening to music	Slow breathing
Playing an instrument	Counting to 10
	Smiling
	Laughing out loud
	Taking a break (staying in bed for 20 minutes)

Practice *willingness* by accepting whatever emotions you are experiencing in that moment and not wishing that you feel differently than you do. For the most part, you should choose to engage in healthy activities that are consistent with your values (not activities that you hope will alter your internal experiences).

The ideal deliberate action should (a) have value to you, (b) help you accomplish something, or (c) be fun to do. Use the Putting It Into Action Worksheet (Worksheet 20-4) to record instances throughout the next two weeks in which you are aware of an emotion and respond in either an adaptive (through deliberate action) or nonadaptive (through eating) way.

Skill Builder for Session 20

Complete the following assignments before the next session:

☐ *Activity*: Exercise (e.g., brisk walking) for 45 minutes × 5 days. Record type and minutes on your Keeping Track Form (note that this is an increase from last session).

☐ *Behavior*: Complete the Identifying Triggers of Overeating Worksheet (Worksheet 20-1) and the Rate Your Emotional Eating Worksheet (Worksheet 20-2).

Complete Weekly Review sheet (Appendix D) in the off-week(s) between now and the next session.

☐ *Calories*: Follow a diet that is consistent with your calorie goal. Total the calories for each day (and for the week), calculate a seven-day average, and compare results to your calorie target.

☐ *Days Recorded*: Record every day.

☐ *Experiential Exercise*: Complete the Healthy Behaviors I Will Choose in Response to Difficult Emotions Worksheet (Worksheet 20-3) and the Putting It Into Action Worksheet (Worksheet 20-4).

☐ *Reminder*: Complete your Check-In sheet before the next session. Also, don't forget to bring your Keeping Track Forms (or printout that includes foods, time eaten, and calories) and Home Weight Change Record.

Instructions: Complete the items below *before* you attend Session 21.

A. *Activity*:

Week 1: I exercised on _____ days, for an average of _____ minutes per day.

Week 2: I exercised on _____ days, for an average of _____ minutes per day.

(The goal for last week was 5 × 45 minutes of activity.)

B. *Behavior*:

I did/did not (*circle one*) complete the Identifying Triggers for Overeating Worksheet.

I did/did not (*circle one*) complete the Rate Your Emotional Eating Worksheet.

I did/did not (*circle one*) complete the Weekly Review at home last week.

C. *Calories*:

My daily calorie goal was _____ and my daily calorie average was

Week 1: _____ calories

Week 2: _____ calories

D. *Days Recorded*:

I recorded my intake for _____ of the past 14 days.

E. *Experiential Exercise*:

I did/did not (*circle one*) complete the Healthy Behaviors I Will Choose in Response to Difficult Emotions Worksheet.

I did/did not (*circle one*) complete the Putting It Into Action Worksheet.

CHAPTER 21

Session 21: Lapse Versus Relapse and Reversing Small Weight Gains

Goals for This Session

■ To review events of the past weeks and check in about progress
■ To discuss lapses and how to prevent them from turning into relapses
■ To discuss strategies for preventing and reversing small weight gains
■ To discuss assignments for the coming weeks

Lapse Versus Relapse

Take a moment to think about previous success that you may have had with short-term weight loss. Do you have any fears about regain from your current weight losses?

Reflections about weight regain:

_____

_____

_____

_____

Many people worry about regaining weight once they have lost it. You may have even had a prior experience with losing weight in the short term, but then gaining it back. This program is specifically designed to teach you skills to prevent weight regain in the long term. In other words, the skills learned in this program will help you prevent lapses from turning into relapses. A *lapse* is a single event that is relatively easy to change or reverse. A lapse, when related to weight control, could be considered any unplanned behavior that is a threat to your weight control. For example, a lapse could mean that you skipped recording lunch or you ate a cookie when you had already met your calorie goal for the day. Weight loss is a difficult and extended process, and because of this, it is expected that you will experience a lapse at some point. The most important goal that you can set for yourself is to prevent a lapse from becoming a relapse. A *relapse* is a bigger sequence of events (or string of lapses) that requires more effort to reverse. For example, a relapse might mean not recording your food intake for several days or not engaging in physical activity for the whole week. There are several steps that you can take to prevent lapses from turning into relapses. Strategies for responding to relapses, should they occur, will be discussed later in this session.

First, it is important to *identify the lapse*. There are two methods of doing so. One is to develop a heightened awareness of your behavior. In other words, it is important to catch yourself when you have stopped engaging in an important weight control behavior (e.g., walking, self-monitoring, menu planning, food logging, weighing, or low-calorie eating). It can be difficult to detect some of these behaviors in the hectic shuffle of everyday life. However, it can sometimes be helpful to stop and ask yourself, "If I kept doing this [not recording, having dessert, not exercising] each day for a month, would I begin to gain weight?" If the answer is yes, then you have lapsed from your weight control program and should employ strategies to get back on track. Another method of identifying your lapse is noticing a small weight gain. Small weight gains generally indicate that you have stopped adhering to some of your weight control goals. Reversing small weight gains will be discussed later in this session.

Second, it is important *determine the cause* of the lapse. Consider what factors may have led you to lapse recently (or in the past).

Factors leading to lapse:

_____

_____

_____

_____

There are several types of factors that can lead to lapses. See Table 21-1 for the types of factors and examples.

Once the cause of the lapse has been determined, you should use that information *to identify high-risk situations for the future.* Recall previous slips or lapses and reflect on what was happening at that time. What events led to the lapse? Some circumstances are commonly found to be high-risk scenarios for lapses during weight management. For example, emotional situations, positive and negative alike, can be challenging. Some types of high-risk situations may come up more often for you than others. Nonetheless, review each high-risk situation in Worksheet 21-1 and evaluate whether it may present a risk for you. Circle any examples that may be a challenge for you. If you identify a situation that presents a risk for lapse that is not on this list, add it to the list in the space provided.

Once these high-risk situations have been identified, you can create a plan to use in such situations to prevent lapse. Everyone has high-risk situations; those who are able to implement plans to deal with them before they turn into lapses are more likely to be successful. It is important to write this plan down so that you can refer to it the midst of a slip. A well-developed plan includes making changes to one or more of the following areas: the situation, your thoughts, and your behaviors. Last, you will be more likely to follow your plan when you need it if it is specific and detailed. For your Skill Builder you will complete the My Behavioral

Table 21-1 Factors Affecting Lapses

Type of Cause	Examples
Proximal	▪ Reduced Keeping Track Form logging
	▪ Reduced menu planning
	▪ Reduced physical activity
	▪ Change in mood
Distal	▪ Stressful life circumstances
	▪ Conflict in relationships
	▪ Loss or setback
Psychological	▪ Mindless decision-making
	▪ Lowered commitment
	▪ Lowered willingness to experience cravings, emotions, loss of pleasure

Action Plan for High-Risk Situations Worksheet (Worksheet 21-2) and the My Psychological Action Plan for High-Risk Situations Worksheet (Worksheet 21-3).

Preventing and Reversing Small Weight Gains

Preventing and reversing small weight gains is a principal skill of long-term weight control. Like lapses, small weight gains are unavoidable in the course of weight management. No one, regardless of his or her level of commitment, has weight stability forever. While small weight gains may be inevitable, they are not signs that your effort is pointless. Small weight gains do not have to be obstacles; it is how you respond to them that matters. Because weight gain can be upsetting, it is useful to have a structured plan (developed ahead of time) to follow to help get back on track.

The most critical component of this plan is self-monitoring of weight. You should weigh yourself at least weekly and record the weight. Daily weighing is likely helpful, but more than once daily is discouraged. Weight gain is of special concern when it reflects a trajectory of increasing weight over time. *A weight gain of 3 to 5 pounds should be taken seriously before it becomes larger.* The weight that is 3 to 5 pounds above your current weight is your "Red Zone" weight. Take a moment to record your current weight and calculate your Red Zone weight.

- Your Current Weight: _____ pounds
- Your Red Zone weight: _____ pounds (3–5 lbs. above current weight)

If you are using a graph to track your weight (Appendix C), it can be helpful to denote your Red Zone on the graph so you can identify it quickly and easily. See Figure 21-1 for an example of marking the Red Zone weight.

Use the blank Weight Graph (Appendix C in your workbook) to graph your current weight and mark your Red Zone. Note that as you lose weight, your Red Zone will also move downward. See Figure 21-2 for an example of how the Red Zone can move.

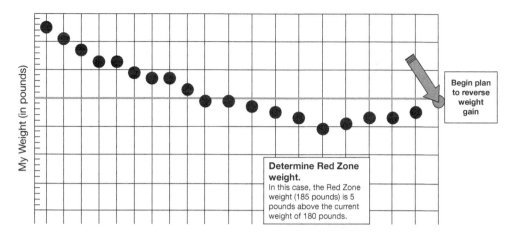

Figure 21-1

Example of Graphing Red Zone Weight

Note that the Red Zone does *not* move when you gain weight. If your weight gain has reached the Red Zone, a plan for reversing small weight gains should be executed.

There are a few key "control what you can" strategies that should be added to your plan (in addition to weighing yourself frequently). First, plans should incorporate self-monitoring (and modifying) your food intake and physical activity. If you are not recording at the time when you are enacting your plan, it is strongly recommended that you go back to recording what you are eating to increase your awareness of any problem areas. Your recordings should include the time, description of amount, and calories consumed. Remember to write down everything you eat and drink as soon as possible after you consumed the items. You might also think

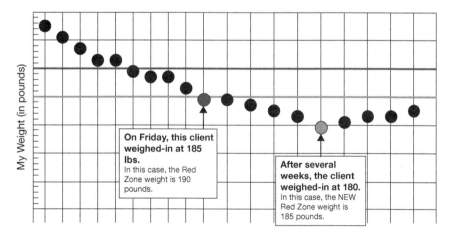

Figure 21-2

Example of Moving Red Zone Weight

about including a concrete, doable calorie goal in your plan. In your plan, you might even consider noting some specific changes that you will make to accomplish the calorie goal (e.g., decrease amount of sauces and butter by one-third, eating a snack before leaving work). Plans should also include increasing (or starting) physical activity. Be sure to set a goal for the type of activity, time (minutes), and number of days per week. See Table 21-2 for suggestions of behavioral strategies that can be most helpful for responding to small weight gains. Check off suggestions that you will include in your plan for reversing small weight gains.

In addition to "control what you can" strategies, you should consider utilizing some "accept what you can't" strategies in your plan for reversing small weight gains. During times when weight control is not going particularly well, you should be aware of thoughts and feelings that may lead you to avoid weighing yourself or self-monitoring food/activity. Consider

Table 21-2 Responding to Small Weight Gains: Control What You Can

Check off any behavioral strategies that you will include in your plan for reversing small weight gains.

☐ **Engineer your environment** and keep tempting, high-calorie foods out of the house

☐ **Stock your home with healthy foods** that you want to be featured in your diet

☐ **Keep healthy foods on hand** when you are out of the house (e.g., traveling, at work, running errands)

☐ **Limit frequency of eating in restaurants or fast-food outlets**; when you do go, use restaurant eating strategies (e.g., plan ahead, choose restaurants wisely, ask for what you want, portion control)

☐ **Have a plan for eating**, rather than going out "into the wild" without one

☐ **Buy foods in portion-controlled servings** or use baggies or Tupperware to make portion-controlled servings

☐ **Use portion control:** serve yourself only how much you intend to eat (avoid family-style serving)

☐ **Grocery shop wisely** (e.g., use lists, meal plans, online ordering, avoid certain sections of store)

☐ **Ask for support** from people who influence your eating

☐ Place sneakers, workout clothes, gear, notes, or pictures in a **visible location as a reminder to exercise**

☐ **Keep a calendar** visible to plan/keep track of physical activity

☐ **Limit TV** watching and screen time

☐ **Limit sitting time** (i.e., sedentary behaviors) at home or at work

thoughts that you might have that would make it difficult to step on the scale.

Thoughts about weighing yourself:

_____

_____

_____

_____

Similar to other distressing thoughts and feelings that you have dealt with thus far in the program, you might consider using psychological strategies to distance yourself from these experiences and act in accordance with your values. For instance, you can use defusion strategies such as "I am having the thoughts that . . ." or changing "but" to "and." Try to use a defusion strategy to gain distance from the thoughts that you wrote here. Describe what strategy you are using and what your new response will be to those thoughts or feelings.

Defusing from thoughts about weighing yourself:

_____

_____

_____

_____

Furthermore, it may be helpful to practice willingness by stepping on the scale (e.g., pursuing the value of health), even when some part of your mind does not want to. See Table 21-3 for a review of psychological strategies that you can incorporate into your plan for reversing small weight gains.

You will make your own plan for reversing small weight gains for the Skill Builder this week. Using the My Plan for Reversing a Small Weight Gain Worksheet (Worksheet 21-4), include two or three behavioral and psychological strategies from Tables 21-2 and 21-3. Your plan should be specific and sufficiently intensive to reverse a small weight gain. Even though you may not be in the Red Zone now, this exercise is important because these plans tend to work the best when formulated ahead of time, when you are not already in distress because of a weight gain.

Table 21-3 Responding to Small Weight Gains: Using "Accept What You Can" Strategies

Core Skill	Description
Acceptance	Acceptance means to embrace thoughts and feelings (even when uncomfortable) without trying to minimize/avoid/change them.
Willingness	Willingness means choosing behaviors that move you toward your values/goals, in spite of the internal experiences that may result (e.g., having a less pleasurable experience).
Flexibility	The goal of these psychological strategies is flexibility. When you are open to any internal experience (including those that are uncomfortable or less pleasurable), you have the freedom to engage in the behaviors that are most consistent with what you value.
Defusion	Defusion means to get distance ("uncouple") from your internal experiences. This helps you act independently of them. Examples of ways to defuse are to transform your "only if" responses to "even if" responses and to label your internal experiences for what they are (e.g., "I'm having the thought that . . .").
Clarify and commit to values	Know what is important to you in life (i.e., your values). Use reminders (post-its, mottos you repeat) to keep these values in mind, including health-related values. Recommit to your values regularly. Remind yourself what you want your life to be about.
Mindful decision-making	The mind often makes decisions without you being aware due to unconscious processes. Be mindful of your decisions about eating and activity. Make each choice a vote for your values. Remember to slow down, pay deliberate attention, stop and think, and take control of your decision.
Control what you can; accept what you can't	Accept food environments that can't be changed. Accept your internal experiences that make weight control difficult. Take control of the part of your food environment that you can change (e.g., in your house). Take control of your *behaviors*.

Skill Builder for Session 21

Complete the following assignments before the next session:

☐ *Activity*: Exercise (e.g., brisk walking) for 50 minutes × 5 days (which is an increase from last session). Record type and minutes on your Keeping Track Form.

☐ *Behavior*: Complete the My Behavioral Action Plan for High-Risk Situations Worksheet (Worksheet 21-2) and the My Psychological Action Plan for High-Risk Situations Worksheet (Worksheet 21-3).

Complete your Weekly Review sheet (Appendix D) in the off-week(s) between now and the next session.

☐ *Calories*: Follow a diet that is consistent with your calorie goal. Total the calories for each day (and for the week), calculate a seven-day average, and compare results to your calorie target.

☐ *Days Recorded*: Record every day.

☐ *Experiential Exercise*: Complete the My Plan for Reversing a Small Weight Gain Worksheet (Worksheet 21-4).

☐ *Reminder*: Complete your Check-In sheet before the next session. Also, don't forget to bring your Keeping Track Forms (or printout that includes foods, time eaten, and calories) and Home Weight Change Record.

Instructions: Complete the items below *before* you attend Session 22.

A. *Activity*:

   Week 1: I exercised on _____ days, for an average of _____ minutes per day.

   Week 2: I exercised on _____ days, for an average of _____ minutes per day.

   (The goal for last week was 5 × 50 minutes of activity.)

B. *Behavior*:

   I did/did not (*circle one*) complete the My Behavioral Action Plan for High-Risk Situations Worksheet.

   I did/did not (*circle one*) complete the My Psychological Action Plan for High-Risk Situations Worksheet.

   I did/did not (*circle one*) complete the Weekly Review at home last week.

C. *Calories*: My daily calorie goal was _____ and my daily calorie average was

   Week 1: _____ calories

   Week 2: _____ calories

D. *Days Recorded*:

   I recorded my intake for _____ of the past 14 days.

E. *Experiential Exercise*:

   I did/did not (*circle one*) complete the My Plan for Reversing a Small Weight Gain Worksheet.

CHAPTER 22

Session 22: Revisiting Commitment and Transition to Monthly/Bimonthly Meetings

Goals for This Session

- To review events of the past weeks and check in about progress
- To revisit commitment strategies
- To discuss assignments for the coming weeks

Personal Commitment Report

Several months ago you shared a personal commitment with the group. We are interested in whether or not you are keeping this commitment. Please take a minute to complete the following items, depending on whether or not you kept your commitment.

- If you *have* kept it:

    - One key to keeping this commitment has been

    _____.

- If you *have not* kept it:

    - One change I am going to make as part of recommitting is

    _____.

Complete the following assignments before the next session:

☐ *Activity*: Exercise (e.g., brisk walking) for 50 minutes × 5 days. Record type and minutes on your Keeping Track Form.

☐ *Behavior*: Work on the behavioral goal that you identified during today's session (specify goal here):

_____

_____

_____

Complete your Weekly Review sheet (Appendix D) in the off-week(s) between now and the next session.

☐ *Calories*: Follow a diet that is consistent with your calorie goal. Total the calories for each day (and for the week), calculate a seven-day average, and compare results to your calorie target.

☐ *Days Recorded*: Record every day.

☐ *Experiential Exercise*: Complete the Recommitment! Worksheet (Worksheet 22-1).

☐ *Reminder*: Complete your Check-In sheet before the next session. Also, don't forget to bring your Keeping Track Forms (or printout that includes foods, time eaten, and calories) and Home Weight Change Record.

Instructions: Complete the items below *before* you attend Session 23.

A. *Activity*:

Week 1: Last week I exercised on _____ days, for an average of _____ minutes per day.

Week 2: Last week I exercised on _____ days, for an average of _____ minutes per day.

Week 3: Last week I exercised on _____ days, for an average of _____ minutes per day.

Week 4: Last week I exercised on _____ days, for an average of _____ minutes per day.

(The goal for last week was 5 × 50 minutes of activity.)

B. *Behavior*:

The behavioral goal I set in session last week:

_____

_____

_____

I did/did not *(circle one)* achieve my behavioral goal.

I did/did not *(circle one)* complete the Weekly Review at home last week.

C. *Calories*:

My daily calorie goal was _____ and my daily calorie average was

Week 1: _____ calories.

Week 2: _____ calories.

Week 3: _____ calories.

Week 4: _____ calories.

D. *Days Recorded* I recorded my intake for _____ of the past 30 days.

E. *Experiential Exercise*:

I did/did not *(circle one)* complete the Recommitment! Worksheet.

CHAPTER 23

Session 23: Maintaining Motivation

Goals for This Session

- To review events of the past weeks and check in about progress
- To discuss strategies for maintaining motivation
- To discuss assignments for the coming weeks

Maintaining Motivation

You have acquired a lot of knowledge of diet and physical activity throughout the course of this program. Although this knowledge is necessary for successful weight control, it is not sufficient; *motivation* to maintain the lifestyle changes is also critical.

Maintaining motivation for lifestyle changes such as being physically active, self-monitoring, and eating a diet that is consistent with your calorie target can be especially challenging during the weight loss maintenance phase. Motivation may diminish during weight maintenance for a couple of reasons.

- The process of losing weight can be very reinforcing and rewarding. Seeing the number drop on the scale each week, receiving attention from others for weight loss, or dropping one size per month can be powerful motivators to maintain lifestyle changes that promote weight loss. Once you are working on weight loss maintenance, however, many of these motivators are no longer be present, at least not to the same degree. As a result, motivation to continue to engage in the behaviors that are necessary to maintain your weight loss may be lower.

- Weight regain tends to occur slowly and the negative consequences of weight gain may not be immediately noticeable. It can therefore be difficult to remain motivated to avoid engaging in unhealthy habits that contribute to weight gain and to instead continue engaging in healthy behaviors (which may be less pleasurable or more effortful). For example, a person may begin to eat out more frequently on the weekends with the rationale that "one more meal out won't hurt," when in fact the extra calories consumed while eating out are subtly contributing to weight regain.

Engaging in weight maintenance over the long term is difficult, and, as discussed above, people often lose motivation. It is therefore important to find ways to maintain motivation to engage in healthy lifestyle behaviors over the long term. Staying focused on your values is one of the best ways to do this.

As has been discussed in previous sessions, in many ways, your weight loss journey is like driving a bus on a highway toward your values. As you continue to drive down the highway to weight loss maintenance and a healthy lifestyle, you are carrying a number of bothersome "passengers" with you. These "passengers" are the thoughts, feelings, urges, and other internal experiences that make long-term weight control difficult. Unfortunately, we know of no way to get these bothersome "passengers" off the bus. Thus, you have a choice to either continue driving down the highway toward your values, accepting that these passengers are along for the ride, or you can pull over and stop making progress.

At this point in the program, you have learned the skills necessary to continue driving toward a healthy lifestyle. One of the best ways to maintain motivation to continue using the strategies that you have learned and to keep driving down the highway is to "keep your eyes on the compass." A compass can tell you if you are moving in the direction of what you value (e.g., long-term health), or if you have veered off course. Keeping your values in the forefront of your minds and staying mindful of why you want to keep moving down the highway will help you to stay motivated to continue making progress, even with those bothersome "passengers" along for the ride. Values make the hard work of willingness worth it.

In the spaces below, identify some of the values that motivate you to engage in the hard work of healthy living.

Ex. Being a positive, healthy role model for my family

1. _____

2. _____

3. _____

4. _____

5. _____

After you have identified the values that make the hard work of weight control worth it, you can use several strategies to stay aware of and connected to these values. Strategies for remaining aware of and connected to your values include:

- *Visual reminders of your values.* Place visual reminders such as post-it notes, letters/emails to yourself, pictures, meaningful fridge magnets, or symbolic jewelry in your day-to-day environment (i.e., car, work, home, bathroom, etc.) to help remind you of the things that you care about most about.

- *View every decision as a vote for or against your value.* As discussed with regard to mindful decision-making, every decision you make can be viewed as a vote for or against what you care most about. Engage in behaviors that are consistent with your values and that keep you moving down the highway of healthy living.

- *Remember the Rocky Path metaphor.* Think about the journey to a healthy lifestyle as being similar to climbing a rocky mountain path. By being willing to experience the difficulty of walking through the rocks, you will eventually make it to the top of the mountain to enjoy the beautiful view. Similarly, by being willing to experience the difficulties related to weight control such as a loss of pleasure, cravings, or urges, you are moving in the direction of your goals and values related to maintaining a healthy weight and lifestyle.

As part of the Skill Builder this week, you will practice strategies for remaining motivated to work towards your values using the Visual Reminders to Stay Motivated Worksheet (Worksheet 23-1) and the Are You Voting for What You Value? Worksheet (Worksheet 23-2).

Skill Builder for Session 23

Complete the following assignments before the next session:

☐ *Activity*: Exercise (e.g., brisk walking) for 50 minutes × 5 days. Record type and minutes on your Keeping Track Form.

☐ *Behavior*: Work on the behavioral goal that you identified during today's session (specify goal here):

_____

_____

_____

Complete your Weekly Review sheet (Appendix D) in the off-week(s) between now and the next session.

☐ *Calories*: Follow a diet that is consistent with your calorie goal. Total the calories for each day (and for the week), calculate a seven-day average, and compare results to your calorie target.

☐ *Days Recorded*: Record every day.

☐ *Experiential Exercise*: Complete the Visual Reminders to Stay Motivated Worksheet (Worksheet 23-1) and the Are You Voting for What You Value? Worksheet (Worksheet 23-2).

☐ *Reminder*: Complete your Check-In sheet before the next session. Also, don't forget to bring your Keeping Track Forms (or printout that includes foods, time eaten, and calories) and Home Weight Change Record.

Session 24 ABCDE Check-In

Instructions: Complete the items below *before* you attend Session 24.

A. *Activity*:

Week 1: Last week I exercised on _____ days, for an average of _____ minutes per day.

Week 2: Last week I exercised on _____ days, for an average of _____ minutes per day.

Week 3: Last week I exercised on _____ days, for an average of _____ minutes per day.

Week 4: Last week I exercised on _____ days, for an average of _____ minutes per day.

(The goal for last week was 5 × 50 minutes of activity.)

B. *Behavior*:

The behavioral goal I set in session last week:

_____

_____

_____.

I did/did not (*circle one*) achieve my behavioral goal.

I did/did not (*circle one*) complete the Weekly Review each week.

C. *Calories*:

My daily calorie goal was _____ and my daily calorie average was

Week 1: _____ calories. **Week 2:** _____ calories.

Week 3: _____ calories. **Week 4:** _____ calories.

D. *Days Recorded*:

I recorded my intake for _____ of the past 30 days.

E. *Experiential Exercise*:

I did/did not (*circle one*) complete the Visual Reminders to Stay Motivated Worksheet.

I did/did not (*circle one*) complete the Are You Voting for What You Value? Worksheet.

Goals for This Session

- To review events of the past weeks and check in about progress
- To review the key behaviors for long-term success
- To review behavioral strategies for implementing key behaviors
- To review psychological strategies for implementing key behaviors
- To discuss assignments for the coming weeks

Looking Ahead: Behavioral and Psychological Keys for Success

The program will be ending after next session. You may feel disappointed or anxious about losing the support of the program and group members. Or you may feel ready to move on and pursue weight loss maintenance on your own. Any of these feelings (or a mixture of them) is perfectly natural at this stage. It is important to recognize your progress and realize that you are ready to independently pursue weight loss maintenance as the next step in your weight control journey. The purpose of this session is to help you plan for your weight control future.

There are several key behaviors that will maximize your future weight control success. Use the Keys to My Long-Term Success Worksheet (Worksheet 24-1) to guide the review of your core strategies for maintaining the key behaviors for weight control success. In the following section, we review these strategies.

Key Behavior 1: Self-Monitor Your Weight

Behavioral Strategies for Self-Monitoring Your Weight

You should be weighing yourself at least once a week to help you stay aware of your eating behaviors and to catch any small weight gains before they become larger weight gains. In the weight loss maintenance phase, many people find it helpful to weigh themselves more often than once a week, up to once a day. There is no "correct" frequency of weighing yourself, as long as it is at least once weekly and not more than once per day. Weighing yourself more than once a day can lead to readings that do not reflect any true changes in weight; rather, changes throughout the day can merely reflect changes in hydration levels or normal digestive variations, for example. Two key strategies for self-monitoring your weight include keeping your scale in a visible location (rather than tucked away in a cabinet or closet) and graphing your weight using one of the weight tracking methods shown in Appendix C, in order to see your weight trends over time. Stay aware of your Red Zone weight (i.e., 3–5 lbs. above your maintenance weight). If you do reach your Red Zone, implement the plan you created in Session 21 to reverse the weight gain as soon as possible.

Psychological Strategies for Self-Monitoring Your Weight

Certain thoughts, feelings, and sensations can lead to avoidance of weighing yourself. Some examples include thoughts such as "I'll wait until I've changed my eating to see my weight" or "It's better not to know" and feelings such as anxiety, dread, and guilt. Although in the short term avoiding the scale may alleviate uncomfortable thoughts and feelings, avoiding the scale may actually intensify these experiences in the long term. In addition, not weighing yourself may prevent you from doing behaviors that are crucial to your long-term values (e.g., health). Instead of responding to thoughts and feelings with avoidance, remember to use *acceptance* and *willingness* to help you weigh yourself even when it is difficult.

1. *Acceptance* is the mental stance of embracing thoughts and feelings related to self-monitoring your weight (even when uncomfortable) without trying to avoid/minimize/change them, and *willingness* is the act of actually weighing yourself despite uncomfortable internal experiences.

2. *What to remember about acceptance*: Distressing thoughts, feelings, sensations, urges, memories, and so on are a part of being human. If your agenda is to eliminate these thoughts and feelings related to self-monitoring your weight, then you will probably become stuck and likely end up avoiding weighing yourself. In fact, attempts to get rid of these thoughts and feelings only exacerbate their intensity and control over your life. This is the same idea as driving the bus and spending all of your time and energy struggling with the passengers so that you don't end up moving in the direction that you want to go. Also, being accepting of distressing thoughts and feelings does not mean that you have to like them or want to have them; rather, it is the stance of realizing that distressing thoughts and feelings are a part of human life and come along with pursuing your values.

3. *What to remember about willingness*: Willingness means making choices because you want the outcome of those choices—because willingness moves you toward what you value—even if those choices mean that you are going to experience difficult thoughts/feelings. It is hard to do! In the Passengers on the Bus metaphor, willingness meant continuing to drive down the road toward your values despite the unpleasantness of the passengers yelling at you to stop. In short, you can choose to step on the scale even if you feel fearful or hopeless and have the thought "It's not that important."

Key Behavior 2: Limit Your Calorie Intake

To maintain a weight that is lower than the weight you were at when you started the program, your calorie intake must stay lower than it was before you started the program. Going back to old eating patterns after a significant weight loss will cause weight gain.

Behavioral Strategies for Limiting Calorie Intake

Remember the following strategies for keeping your calorie intake within your goal:

1. *Self-monitor your calorie intake* (in some form, with some regularity). People will vary in how much they continue to self-monitor after the program ends; however, most individuals who are successful in the long term self-monitor in some way or another. Even if you decide not

to self-monitor moving forward, self-monitoring should be your first go-to behavior if you experience a small weight gain or a lapse.

2. *Limit portion sizes.* Potion sizes have grown dramatically in recent years, and food is sold in large quantities, which can facilitate over-eating. Implement strategies such as avoiding buying in bulk, using small plates, and putting leftovers away before sitting down to eat a meal. You may wish to purchase food in individual servings or to preportion food into baggies or containers right after purchase. Read nutrition labels, and measure and weigh food periodically to make sure your portion sizes are not drifting.

3. *Limit access to high-calorie foods in your home.* We humans are hard-wired to want to eat good-tasting, high-calorie food when it is present. Make access to such food as difficult as possible by not keeping it in the home or by putting such food in places (e.g., the back of the top cabinet) that are not immediately visible.

4. *Grocery shop according to a meal plan.* Stock up on the healthy foods you want to eat frequently. Plan out meal and snack options for the week and shop according to this plan. Healthy foods should be easily accessible and visible (e.g., a fruit bowl on the kitchen table).

5. *Limit restaurant/fast food eating.* Restaurants serve large portions of high-calorie food, and thus excessive restaurant eating should be avoided. If you do decide to eat out, you should try to look up the menu online, choose establishments that publish calorie information, and/or have a portion of your meal boxed up as soon as it is brought to the table to limit unintended overeating. Also, limit alcohol intake in order to prevent intake of excess calories from both alcohol and from mindless eating that can occur after drinking alcohol.

6. *Plan ahead.* In our toxic food environment, a person must constantly exercise self-control to make healthy eating choices. Constantly exercising self-control can become exhausting and may leave too much room for error. Do not count on being able to make healthy decisions in the heat of the moment (e.g., when wait staff circulate with trays of hors d'oeuvres at a party or when you smell donuts on the way to work). Instead, arm yourself with a plan ahead of time (e.g., eating before going to the party; choosing a walking route that does not take you past the donuts shop).

7. *Ask for support* from others who influence what food is available at home, work, and other settings.

Psychological Strategies for Limiting Calorie Intake

Behavioral strategies such as self-monitoring, planning ahead, and controlling your food environment are key for limiting calorie intake, but these strategies may not be quite enough in the long term, especially in challenging situations such as social or work events. *Mindful decision-making* may be useful when you are faced with a tempting food or situations that you cannot prevent. Our minds often make decisions without us being aware (especially when we are distracted, emotional, or in the presence of delicious food). Mindless food decisions are often those that lead to eating large portions of high-calorie foods. The following mindful decision-making strategies may be particularly helpful when controlling the food environment is not possible:

1. *"Stop, think."* You can slow down and pay deliberate attention to both internal (e.g., thoughts, feelings) and external (e.g., smells, sights of foods) cues driving your desire to eat. Heightened awareness of these cues allows you to make a more conscious eating choice.
2. Practice being the *sports commentator* for the process of eating. Acting as a sports commentator brings to awareness every small step that leads to the decision of eating.
3. Make every decision a *vote for or against* life values. For example, does eating a cookie at the party take you closer or farther from your ultimate value of being a healthy grandparent? The ability to carefully consider each eating decision in the context of your most important values will help you decrease mindless eating.

Key Behavior 3: Engage in High Levels of Physical Activity

You should aim to complete 250 minutes of moderate to vigorous physical activity per week in the long term to prevent weight regain. Remember, you can choose to divide the 250 minutes across the week as you please (we recommend 50 minutes a day five days a week), but activity should take place in at least 10-minute bouts in order to get the cardiovascular benefits of exercise. Brisk walking is a particularly good way to get in your activity, as there are fewer barriers that can get in the way. However, you may wish to have several different exercise options to prevent getting bored with your exercise routine.

Behavioral Strategies for Engaging in Physical Activity

1. *Reduce television watching*, as the television serves as a cue to stay sedentary. However, you may choose to exercise while watching TV (e.g., at the gym or while on a treadmill in your living room).

2. *Surround yourself with others who are active*, so they can serve as cues to exercise and become activity partners to keep you accountable.

3. *Put workout items or reminders in a visible place* (e.g., schedule workouts on a daily calendar, put notes in the car, put gym clothes in a visible location). Aim to treat plans to exercise like an appointment for work or with a friend that you would not normally cancel or reschedule.

4. *Include movement in your daily routine* (e.g., park farther away from the office, get off the bus a stop early, walk on the treadmill or outside when having a conversation with a friend, or change a weekly work meeting to a walking meeting).

Psychological Strategies for Engaging in Physical Activity

Although many psychological strategies can help you engage in physical activity, *willingness* and *defusion* can be particularly helpful for engaging in physical activity in the long term. When motivation drops, you can get distance from thoughts and feelings that drive you to not exercise and then engage in the behavior anyway. Strategies for increasing willingness include the following:

1. *Practice labeling thoughts as thoughts.* For example, instead of saying "I do not want to get out of bed and exercise," you can say, "I am having the thought that I do not want to get out of bed and exercise." Labeling thoughts as thoughts allows you the *flexibility* to choose a behavior that is at odds with thoughts and feelings.

2. *Acknowledge your mind for doing its job with "thank you, mind."* For example, you can thank your mind for doing its job when it tells you, "Leave your workout clothes at home today—you deserve a break." Acknowledging the mind's innate desire to keep you at rest can allow for the freedom to choose to be active despite the mind's hard-wired desires.

3. *Separate the thought from behavior by substituting "and" for "but."* For example, instead of saying "I should go to the gym right now, *but* I am so tired," you can say "I should go to the gym right now, *and*

I am so tired." This subtle change in language separates the behavior of going to the gym from the internal experience of feeling tired; feeling tired does not necessitate *not* going to the gym. Instead, you have the option to exercise even if you are feeling tired.

4. *Practice the "Just Do It" method.* You can feel a negative feeling (e.g., dread of exercise, tiredness) and have the thought of not wanting to exercise while doing it anyway.

Key Behavior 4: Stay Mindful of Values to Stay Motivated

Keeping up weight control behaviors in the long term is difficult, so *motivation* is key. However, motivation can decrease, especially during weight maintenance, as keeping off weight is less rewarding than losing weight. Controlling the food environment should make it easier for you to engage in healthy eating even when your motivation wanes. But in challenging moments, motivation will remain essential for maintaining other key behaviors. You can prepare for these challenges by reflecting often on your values. What do you want your life to be about? What do you want to be able to do in the years to come? You may wish to use reminders (e.g., post-its, pictures) to keep your values at the forefront of your mind.

Remember, you should expect to continue working on weight control behaviors in the long term in the same way that you keep up maintenance on your car or at home. For example, you cannot do one spring cleaning per year and expect your house to stay clean without daily straightening, weekly mopping, and so on.

Skill Builder for Session 24

Complete the following assignments before the next session:

☐ *Activity*: Exercise (e.g., brisk walking) for 50 minutes × 5 days. Record type and minutes on your Keeping Track Form.

☐ *Behavior*: Work on the behavioral goal that you identified during today's session (specify goal here):

_____

_____

_____

Complete your Weekly Review sheet (Appendix D) in the off-week(s) between now and the next session.

☐ *Calories*: Follow a diet that is consistent with your calorie goal. Total the calories for each day (and for the week), calculate a seven-day average, and compare results to your calorie target.

☐ *Days Recorded*: Record every day.

☐ *Experiential Exercise*: Complete the Keys to my Long-Term Success Worksheet (Worksheet 24-1).

☐ *Reminder*: Complete your Check-In sheet before the next session. Also, don't forget to bring your Keeping Track Forms (or printout that includes foods, time eaten, and calories) and Home Weight Change Record.

Instructions: Complete the items below *before* you attend Session 25.

A. *Activity*:

Week 1: I exercised on _____ days, for an average of _____ minutes per day.

Week 2: I exercised on _____ days, for an average of _____ minutes per day.

Week 3: I exercised on _____ days, for an average of _____ minutes per day.

Week 4: I exercised on _____ days, for an average of _____ minutes per day.

Week 5: I exercised on _____ days, for an average of _____ minutes per day.

Week 6: I exercised on _____ days, for an average of _____ minutes per day.

Week 7: I exercised on _____ days, for an average of _____ minutes per day.

Week 8: I exercised on _____ days, for an average of _____ minutes per day.

(The goal for last week was 5×50 minutes of activity for each week.)

B. *Behavior*:

The behavioral goal I set in session last week:

_____

_____

_____

I did/did not *(circle one)* achieve my behavioral goal.

I did/did not *(circle one)* complete the Weekly Review each week.

C. *Calories*:

My daily calorie goal was _____ and my daily calorie average was

Week 1: _____ calories.

Week 2: _____ calories.

Week 3: _____ calories.

Week 4: _____ calories.

Week 5: _____ calories.

Week 6: _____ calories.

Week 7: _____ calories.

Week 8: _____ calories.

D. *Days Recorded*

I recorded my intake for _____ days in the past eight weeks.

E. *Experiential Exercise:* I did/did not *(circle one)* complete the Keys to my Long-Term Success Worksheet.

CHAPTER 25 Session 25: Celebrating Accomplishments

- To review events of the past weeks and check in on progress
- To review key strategies that will assist in long-term weight maintenance
- To recognize accomplishments made throughout the course of the program

Celebrating Your Progress

We want to recognize all of your hard work and celebrate the progress you have made! You have made significant changes in your eating and physical activity over the course of the program. You did the work day in and day out to accomplish so much. It can be scary to have sessions end, but you have all of the tools you need to be successful on your own. You have come a long way and deserve a huge amount of credit for making both big and small changes to your life!

Here are some final reminders about the most important parts of weight control:

1. We strongly encourage you to *weigh yourself at least once a week.*

2. *Self-monitoring calorie intake* is perhaps the best weight management tool of all. Writing down everything you are eating and drinking will help you notice when your caloric intake starts to increase and help you get back on track when (not "if") you experience a lapse. You will see that a problem is starting before the scale starts to go up too far. Be creative in how you monitor yourself. You may want to continue recording every day, or you may want to record your intake only during high-risk situations (like certain times of day or during special events). Do what works best for you!

3. *Continue or increase your physical activity.* Physical activity is one of the most helpful strategies to help maintain your weight loss and is an essential part of weight control.

4. *Check in about your weight control progress.* We recommend doing this by continuing to do your Weekly Review.

5. *Optimize your personal environment* to make healthy eating and activity as easy and automatic as possible.

6. *Use psychological strategies* learned in this program. For example, stay mindful of your values, be mindful when making decisions, and practice willingness.

Using these tools consistently will help prevent significant weight gain from occurring over time.

Keeping Track Form

Date: _____

Time	Food: Amount and Description	Calories
TOTAL		

Type of Physical Activity	Minutes

Note: Adapted, with permission, from Look AHEAD

In-Session Weight Change Record

Name _____

Weight (vertical axis)

Date (horizontal axis)

Example format of an alternative table format

Date	Weight

Home Weight Change Record

Name _____

Example format of an alternative table format

Date	Weight

Weight

Date

Weekly Review

Instructions: Complete your weekly review at home on your own. This form should be completed during each week that you *do not* attend a program session. Answer the following questions on your own.

Activity

Number of days you exercised this week: _____ days.

Total number of minutes of physical activity this week: _____ minutes, for an average of _____ minutes per day.

(The goal for last week was _____ days × _____ minutes of activity.)

Behavioral Goals

▨ Specific goal for the week:

_____

_____

▨ Did you accomplish your goal this week?   ☐ *Yes*   ☐ *No*
▨ If so, how did you do it? If not, what got in the way?

_____

_____

Calories

Number of days you kept food records this week: _____ days.

My goal was _____ calories per day.

Average daily caloric intake for the week: _____ calories.

Weight

_____ lbs.

My weight increased/decreased (*circle one*) _____ lb(s) from last week.

Appendix E

Worksheets

Worksheet 1-1   Cutting Back on High-Calorie Foods Form   *167*

Worksheet 2-1   Calorie Tracking Example   *168*

Worksheet 2-2   Remember Your Purpose   *169*

Worksheet 3-1   What Meals and Snacks Work for Me   *170*

Worksheet 4-1   Daily Meal Planner   *171*

Worksheet 5-1   Control What You Can, Accept What You Can't   *172*

Worksheet 6-1   Activity Goals   *173*

Worksheet 6-2   Activity Planner   *174*

Worksheet 6-3   Types of Exercise   *175*

Worksheet 6-4   Transforming "Only If . . ." to "Even If . . ." Responses   *178*

Worksheet 6-5   Transforming Your "Only If . . ." to "Even If . . ." Responses at Home   *179*

Worksheet 7-1   Practicing Willingness   *180*

Worksheet 7-2   10 Valued Domains   *181*

Worksheet 8-1   Practicing Flexibility   *185*

Worksheet 8-2   Pattern Smashing Activity   *186*

Worksheet 9-1   Restaurant Eating Tips   *187*

Worksheet 10-1 In Order to Behave Consistently With My Values, I Was Willing to . . .   *189*

Worksheet 12-1 Fusion Versus Defusion   *190*

Worksheet 12-2 Urge Surfing   *191*

Worksheet 13-1 Practicing Defusion   *193*

Worksheet 15-1 Mindful Decision-Making *194*

Worksheet 16-1 Skill Review *195*

Worksheet 17-1 How Do You Compare to the NWCR Members? *196*

Worksheet 17-2 Your Weight Maintenance Plan for Success *197*

Worksheet 17-3 Using Psychological Strategies to Maintain Weight Control Behaviors *198*

Worksheet 18-1 Overcoming Barriers to Physical Activity *199*

Worksheet 19-1 Committed Action *200*

Worksheet 20-1 Identifying Triggers of Overeating *201*

Worksheet 20-2 Rate Your Emotional Eating *202*

Worksheet 20-3 Healthy Behaviors I Will Choose in Response to Difficult Emotions *203*

Worksheet 20-4 Putting It Into Action *204*

Worksheet 21-1 High-Risk Situations *205*

Worksheet 21-2 My Behavioral Action Plan for High-Risk Situations *207*

Worksheet 21-3 My Psychological Action Plan for High-Risk Situations *208*

Worksheet 21-4 My Plan for Reversing a Small Weight Gain *209*

Worksheet 22-1 Recommitment! *210*

Worksheet 23-1 Visual Reminders to Stay Motivated *211*

Worksheet 23-2 Are You Voting for What You Value? *212*

Worksheet 24-1 Keys to My Long-Term Success *213*

Worksheet 25-1 Celebrating Accomplishments *215*

Worksheet 1-1 Cutting Back on High-Calorie Foods Form

Instructions: This week, avoid or cut down (by at least one-third) your intake of the common high-calorie foods listed here. Place a check next to the foods you plan to avoid or cut back your intake of by at least one-third this week.

- ☐ Chips
- ☐ Nuts, buttered popcorn, pretzels, cheese puffs, and other salty snack foods
- ☐ Full-calorie butter or margarine
- ☐ Full-calorie mayonnaise
- ☐ Full-calorie salad dressing
- ☐ Full-calorie soda, lemonade, iced tea, sports drinks, juice drinks
- ☐ Cream or whole milk
- ☐ Cookies, cakes, pies, muffins, donuts
- ☐ Ice cream or other high-calorie frozen desserts
- ☐ Chocolate or candy
- ☐ High-sugar cereal
- ☐ Alcohol (beer, wine, liquor)
- ☐ Cream- or cheese-based dips or spreads

Worksheet 2-1 Calorie Tracking Example

Instructions: Please fill in the missing calorie amounts and total each meal. You will find the completed examples in Figure 2-5 at the end of this chapter—but before you look, try your best to complete these examples on your own.

Meal #1: McDonalds

Food/Beverage	Amount	Calories
Burger with cheese	1- quarter pound burger with cheese	
French fries	1 large serving 5.5 oz	
Milk Shake	16 oz chocolate shake	

TOTAL: _____ Calories

Meal # 2: Prepared at Home

Food/Beverage	Amount	Calories
12-grain bread	2 slices	
Turkey Meat	2 slices Butterball, Sliced, oven-roasted	
Lettuce	¼ cup shredded	
Tomato	⅓ small raw tomato sliced	
Mustard	1 tsp	
Apple	1 medium	
Milk	1 cup skim 8 oz	

TOTAL: _____ Calories

Worksheet 2-2 Remember Your Purpose

◼ Why I joined the program:

_____

_____

_____

_____

_____

_____

◼ What I hope to achieve by taking part in the program:

_____

_____

_____

_____

_____

_____

◼ How losing weight will help me:

_____

_____

_____

_____

_____

_____

Worksheet 3-1 What Meals and Snacks Work for Me

Instructions: Please complete this worksheet about what meals and snacks work for you before the next session. You will share this information with other group members at the next session. You might highlight options that are most convenient, especially satisfying, good tasting, or inexpensive—whatever is working well for you. For example, you might share a favorite recipe, a good bet for a fast-food lunch, or a go-to breakfast. All ideas will be helpful!

	Description	Calories
Breakfast		
Lunch		
Dinner		
Snack		

Worksheet 4-1 Daily Meal Planner

Calorie Target (Total): ___	Breakfast	Lunch	Dinner	Snacks
	Calorie Target (Breakfast): ___	Calorie Target (Lunch): ___	Calorie Target (Dinner): ___	Calorie Target (Snack): ___
Option 1				
Option 2				
Option 3				

Worksheet 5-1 Control What You Can, Accept What You Can't

This week, describe at least one situation when you *accepted* something that you could not change (e.g., urge to overeat, food craving, desire to avoid physical activity) and instead focused your energy on *controlling your behavior*. What was the outcome?

_____

_____

_____

_____

_____

_____

_____

_____

_____

_____

_____

_____

_____

_____

_____

_____

_____

_____

_____

_____

Worksheet 6-1 Activity Goals

Session	Days Per Week	Minutes Per Day	Total Minutes Per Week
1–5	3	15	**45**
6–7	3	20	**60**
8–9	4	20	**80**
10–11	4	25	**100**
12–15	4	30	**120**
16–17	5	30	**150**
18–19	5	40	**200**
20	5	45	**225**
21 and up	5	50	**250**

Worksheet 6-2 Activity Planner

	What I will do	When I will do it	Minutes
Monday			
Tuesday			
Wednesday			
Thursday			
Friday			
Saturday			
Sunday			
		Total minutes of activity:	

Worksheet 6-3 Types of Exercise

We suggest **brisk walking**. It's easy to do and good for you. Here are some other activities that are usually similar to brisk walking:

- Aerobic dance (high impact, low impact, step aerobics)
- Bicycle riding (outdoors or on a stationary bike indoors)
- Dancing (Zumba, square dancing, line dancing). Note: Be careful not to include breaks.
- Hiking
- Jogging (outdoor, indoor, treadmill)
- Karate
- Rope jumping
- Rowing (canoeing)
- Skating (ice skating, roller skating, rollerblading)
- Skiing (downhill, cross-country, Nordic Track)
- Soccer
- StairMaster
- Swimming (laps, snorkeling, scuba diving)
- Tennis
- Volleyball
- Walking (outdoor, indoor at mall, on indoor track at fitness center, treadmill)
- Water Aerobics

Here are some safe and easy stretches:

1. Arm reaches
   *Stand up straight with your feet approximately shoulder-width apart.
   *Count to five as you stretch your right arm to the ceiling, making sure to keep your feet flat on the floor. Lower your right arm and repeat with your left arm.
   *Do this 10 times. When you have completed 10 sets of arm reaches, gently shake out your arms.

2. Arm circles
   *Stand with your feet approximately shoulder-width apart with your knees slightly bent.
   *Extend your arms straight out from the shoulders to the side (left arm out to the left, right arm out to the right) with your fingers spread apart and your palms facing down toward the floor. Keep your buttocks and stomach flexed as your reach out your arms.
   *Rotate your arms in circles forward 10 times. Once you have completed forward circles, rotate your arms backward 10 times. Once you have completed 10 forward and 10 backward arm circles, gently shake out your arms.
   *Gradually work up to performing 20 circles forward and 20 circles backward.

3. Waist bends

    *Stand up tall with your feet approximately shoulder-width apart.

    *While looking straight ahead, bend to the right, bringing your right arm down the side of your body and extending your left arm gently over your head. Count to 10 and then slowly return to the straight-up, standing position.

    *Repeat on the left side (bend to the left, bring your left arm down the side of your body, and extend your right arm over your head).

    *Gradually work up to performing five sets on each side.

4. Sitting toe touch

    *Sit on the floor with your feet placed flat against a wall, legs outstretched, with your knees slightly bent. While sitting, reach out your hands and slowly stretch them toward your toes. Breathe as you reach toward your toes for 10 seconds.

    *Repeat this two or three times.

    *Gradually work up to repeating 10 times.

5. Back press

    *Lie on your back on the floor with your knees bent, your feet flat on the ground, and your hands clasped behind your neck. Take a deep breath and relax.

    *Press your lower back against the floor and tighten your stomach and buttock muscles. This should cause your back to flatten against the floor as the lower part of your pelvis rotates forward slightly.

    *Hold this position for five seconds and then relax your stomach and buttock muscles.

6. Back stretch

    *Lie on your back with your knees bent, your feet flat on the floor, and your arms flat on the floor at your sides. Take a deep breath and relax.

    *Grasp the **back** of one knee (the underside—**not** the top of the knee) with both hands and pull your leg as close to your chest as possible. Keep your other leg bent with your foot on the ground as you do this. Return to the starting position.

    *Repeat with the other leg.

7. Heel cord (Achilles) stretch

    *Stand facing a wall approximately an arm's distance away. Stand with your knees straight (but not locked) and your heels flat on the floor.

*With your hands resting on the wall, allow your body to slowly lean forward by bending your elbows and allowing your forearms to move toward the wall. Keep your legs and body straight and your heels on the floor as you slowly lean forward, noticing the stretch in the back of your ankles.

*Return to the original position and repeat.

8. Calf stretch

*Stand up straight with your feet approximately shoulder-width apart.

*Step forward 1 to 2 feet with your right foot and bend your right knee slightly. Make sure that the front of your knee is in line with the front of your toes (and that your knee does not forward beyond your foot). Keep your left leg relatively straight and your left heel on the floor as you do this. Hold this position for 10 to 20 seconds.

*Return to the original position. Repeat on the left side.

Worksheet 6-4 Transforming "Only If . . ." to "Even If . . ." Responses

Write down one or two "only if" thoughts that you have in the blank spaces in the worksheet.

"Only if . . ."	"Even if . . ."
"I'd be able to go for my daily walk *only if* I could have more energy when I wake up in the morning."	"I am going to go for my daily walk, *even if* I feel like I have no energy when I wake up in the morning."
"I'd be able to meet my calorie goal *only if* my family would stop bringing tempting food into the house."	"I will meet my calorie goal, *even if* my family brings tempting food into the house."
"I would be able to eat a healthy dinner *only if* I didn't have to go to work events at night."	"I will eat a healthy dinner, *even if* I have to go to work events at night."
"I'd be able to meet my calorie goal *only if* I didn't crave chips while I watch TV."	"I will meet my calorie goal, *even if* I crave chips while I watch TV."

Note: This worksheet is for use in session while Worksheet 6-5 is for use at home.

Worksheet 6-5 Transforming Your "Only If . . ." to "Even If . . ." Responses at Home

This week, record at least three instances in which you practiced transforming "only if" responses to "even if" responses to a behavioral goal you found especially challenging:

"Only if . . ."	"Even if . . ."

Try to predict situations in which you might be tempted to *engage in a behavior contrary to your weight control goals* (e.g., eating junk food at a party, skipping your walk when it is raining). At home, record thoughts/feelings/urges you have when faced with each situation and rate your willingness to engage in the weight control behavior, instead of giving in to the temptation, on a scale of 1 to 10. Then record the end behavior that occurred. An example is provided.

Situation	Thoughts/ Feelings/ Urges	Willingness: 1 (lowest) to 10 (highest)	Outcome/Behavior
Coworker brought cookies to work	"Those cookies look really good. One can't hurt." Kept imagining what it would be like to bite into it. Wanted it a lot!	7	Ate an apple instead

Instructions: This exercise will help you decide how you want to *live*. The following 10 domains are examples of areas of life that people value. Some of these domains may not be important to you. If not, do not feel pressured to write something; just skip it and move on the next one.

1. Marriage/Couple/Intimate Relationship

This is the relationship you have with a "significant other." If you are not in such a relationship right now, you can still answer these questions in terms of what you aspire to find in such a relationship.

What kind of person would you most like to be in the context of an intimate relationship? It might help to think about specific actions you would like to take and then use those to dig down to the underlying motives for such actions. What are those underlying motives? How do they reflect what you value in your relationship?

_____

_____

_____

_____

_____

2. Parenting

Think about what it means to you to be a mother or father. What sort of role do you want to have? If you don't have children, you can still answer this question. In what ways is it important to you to support this role in others?

_____

_____

_____

_____

_____

3. Family Relations (other than intimate relations and parenting)

This domain is about family roles beyond those of being a spouse or parent. Think about what it means to be a son, daughter, aunt, uncle, cousin, grandparent, or in-law. What sort of role would you like to have in your family relationships? What values would you like to see in this area of your life?

_____

_____

_____

_____

_____

4. Friendship/Social Relations

What kind of friend would you like to be? Think about your closest friends and see if you can connect with what you would like to experience in your life regarding your friends.

_____

_____

_____

_____

_____

5. Career/Employment

What kind of employee do you most want to be? What do you want to stand for in your work? What kind of a difference do you want to make through your job?

_____

_____

_____

_____

_____

6. Education/Training/Personal Growth and Development

This area includes all the things you do to learn, though it is not necessarily school-based. What type of learner do you want to be? How would you like to engage with that area of your life?

_____

_____

_____

_____

_____

7. Recreation/Leisure

Activities in this area help us recharge and often allow us to connect with family and friends. Think about what is important to you about your hobbies, sports, and other forms of recreation. In these areas, what would you like to have developed in your life?

_____

_____

_____

_____

_____

8. Spirituality

Spirituality includes everything that helps you feel connected to something larger than yourself but does not necessarily have to be connected to organized religion. It includes your faith and spiritual practices. What do you most want to embody in this area of your life?

_____

_____

_____

_____

_____

9. Citizenship

How would you like to contribute to society and be a member of the community? What sort of person do you want to be in the realm of social, political, charitable, and community areas?

_____

_____

_____

_____

_____

10. Health/Physical Well-Being

We are physical beings, and taking care of our bodies and our health through diet, exercise, and sound health practices is another important domain. What is important to you in these areas?

_____

_____

_____

_____

_____

Worksheet 8-1 Practicing Flexibility

Think of two or three bad habits you have related to eating or physical activity. What would be a powerful demonstration of flexibility in relation to these habits? Try out new ways of behaving in response to the same situation, thought, or feeling that are **radically different** from your usual behavior/habit.

Bad habit:

1. _____

_____

_____

2. _____

_____

_____

3. _____

_____

_____

New behaviors:

1. _____

_____

_____

2. _____

_____

_____

3. _____

_____

_____

Worksheet 8-2 Pattern Smashing Activity

Instructions: Most individuals have developed narrow habits that make weight control difficult. Practice pattern smashing instead of continuing with these old habits. Choose at least three habits to use pattern smashing against (i.e., deliberately engaging in a behavior that runs counter to your old pattern of behavior) and record your experience below.

Old Habit	Plan to Pattern Smash	Outcome
Example: Eating a cookie every night after dinner.	Example: Eating a piece of fruit instead of a cookie every night after dinner.	Example: I was able to eat a piece of fruit instead of my usual cookie each night, which made meeting my calorie goal easier!

Worksheet 9-1 Restaurant Eating Tips

Restaurant eating can be a challenge if you are trying to change your eating habits. But don't worry—it is possible to make healthy food choices if you know what to *look* and *ask* for!

The following strategies and questions will help guide you in your future menu selections. Remember, the more questions you ask, the more knowledgeable you become about the food choices and the easier the choice becomes.

1. Plan ahead

- Call ahead of time to ask about low-calorie choices and plan your meal before going to the restaurant.
- "Bank" calories (i.e., eat fewer calories during other meals that day or on the previous day so you have additional calories for your meal out).
- Eat something small before you go to the restaurant to prevent you from being ravenous when you get there.

2. Ask for what you want. Take charge!

- Ask the server *not* to bring the bread, chips, or other "freebies" to the table.
- Ask about the method of preparation. Are they using oil or butter to cook the food?
- If the method of preparation is high in calories, ask if you can modify it to reduce the calories and/or fat. For example, can food be prepared without added fat such as butter or oil?
- Order salad dressing, gravy, sauce, and other spreads that tend to be high in calories "on the side."
- Ask if you can split the meal without an extra charge.
- Consider ordering an appetizer or children's size portion rather than the full-size entree.
- Ask if you can order food à la carte (separately) rather than as a full meal.
- Ask if you can substitute lower calorie items such as a salad or baked potato for high-calorie foods like French fries.
- Look for ways to reduce the amount of high-calorie foods in the entrée. For example, can they put less cheese on the pizza?
- See if the menu offers "light," "low-fat," or healthy items.
- If it isn't listed on the menu, ask if the restaurant has calorie, fat, and portion size information available upon request.
- Ask that your plate be removed from the table as soon as you finish.
- Before or after the meal, put the amount of food that you don't want to eat in a "to go" container to take home.

3. Choose foods carefully

- Think about what parts of the meal are most worth your calories.

4. Limit alcohol

- Drinking alcohol may lead to less control over eating.
- Drinking alcohol also reduces the number of calories that can be spent on food.

5. Use portion control for high-calorie foods. Watch out for these potentially high-calorie words on menus:

- Au gratin	- Hollandaise
- Breaded	- Parmesan
- Buttered, buttery	- Pastry
- Cheese sauce	- Rich
- Creamy, cream sauce	- Sautéed
- Fried (deep-, pan-, batter)	- Scalloped
- Gravy	- Seasoned
- Southern style	

Worksheet 10-1 In Order to Behave Consistently With My Values, I Was Willing to . . .

Instructions: Pay attention this week to the ways in which you make weight-related decisions that are consistent with what you value. Note the behavior you engage in and what you were willing to experience as part of that behavior.

	In order to behave consistently with my values, I engaged in this weight control behavior:	... and I was willing to experience the following emotions, sensations, and/or thoughts:
Example A	Cooking dinner at home instead of going out to eat	Craving restaurant meal, knowing that cooking would take more effort, feeling tired
Example B	Going to the gym in the morning instead of sleeping in	Feeling like I had no energy, having the thought that it would be so much more comfortable and easier to stay in bed
1.		
2.		
3.		

Worksheet 12-1 Fusion Versus Defusion

Instructions: This week, take notice of times when you are fused and defused with your internal experiences (e.g., thoughts, feelings, urges, cravings). Write down at least two times you were fused and two times you were defused and what the behavioral outcome of each was.

Fusion

	Example of Being Fused	Behavioral Outcome
Example	*I craved a slice of cake, so I had to eat it.*	*I ate the slice of cake, which put me 250 calories above my daily calorie goal.*
1.		
2.		

Defusion

	Example of Being Defused	Behavioral Outcome
Example	*I craved a slice of cake and recognized that this was just an internal experience.*	*I chose a piece of fruit instead of the cake, which allowed me to stay within my calorie goal.*
1.		
2.		

Worksheet 12-2 Urge Surfing

Instructions: Choose a situation in which you notice yourself craving something to practice urge surfing (see Session 12 for the guidelines for urge surfing). Answer the following questions regarding your experience of urge surfing:

1. What are the exact thoughts, feelings, or physical sensations in your body?

    _____

    _____

    _____

    _____

    _____

2. Describe the location in your body where the urge exists. Where does it start and where does it stop (i.e., what are its boundaries)?

    _____

    _____

    _____

    _____

    _____

3. What happens when you are open to this internal experience and are not trying to suppress the experience or get rid of it?

    _____

    _____

    _____

    _____

    _____

4. How long does the urge last? Does it come and go? Does it rise, peak, and fall?

_____

_____

_____

_____

_____

Worksheet 13-1 Practicing Defusion

Practice using the following strategies to defuse from "sticky" thoughts, feelings, and urges. Choose several situations in which you find yourself getting stuck to a thought, feeling, or urge, and use a defusion strategy to step back and get some distance from these internal experiences. Record the thought, feeling, or urge that prompted the need for a defusion strategy. Then briefly discuss the behavioral outcome of using the strategy.

	Strategy	Thought/Feeling/Urge	Outcome
Ex.	Label internal experiences: "I'm having the thought that …"	"I have to have the pizza. It's my favorite dish on the menu!"	Decided to get a lower calorie sandwich instead of the pizza (even though I still wanted the pizza).
1	Label internal experiences: "I'm having the thought/feeling/urge that …"		
2	Imagine internal experiences as leaves on a stream that you are watching float by		
3	Uncouple internal experiences (like thoughts or cravings) from behaviors by *using "and" instead of "but"*		
4	Thank your mind/body for the thought/feeling/urge ("thank you, mind!")		
5	"Just do it!" Feel the feeling, think the thought, experience the urge and choose the healthy behavior anyway		

Worksheet 15-1 Mindful Decision-Making

Instructions: Practice mindful decision-making with regard to food and physical activity. For each of the next seven days, choose an eating or activity decision point to practice making mindful eating/activity choices. It can be especially helpful to identify instances in which you might eat mindlessly or make mindless decisions about eating or activity. Use the strategies discussed in group to be especially mindful during the situation. For each day, record the situation, the strategy (stop and think, values vote, slowing, or other) and the outcome.

	Situation	Strategy	Outcome
Ex.	Snacking on ingredients while cooking dinner in the kitchen.	Stop, think!	Paused before continuing to pop food into my mouth and decided to wait until the meal was fully ready and I could sit at the table to eat.
Day 1			
Day 2			
Day 3			
Day 4			
Day 5			
Day 6			
Day 7			

Instructions: Listed below are a few of the psychological skills you have learned up to this point in the program. For each skill, fill in at least one situation for which that strategy has been most helpful for your weight control. Alternatively, list situations where you anticipate the skill *will* be most helpful in the future.

Skill	Situation(s) in which this skill is/will be most helpful
Willingness: Engaging in a valued behavior, regardless of uncomfortable internal experiences.	
Mindful Decision-Making: Stop/think; slowing down the decision-making process; making every eating/physical activity decision an "up" or "down" vote on a value.	
Defusion: A state of distance from your internal experiences so that you can act independently of them (e.g., labeling thoughts/feelings; changing "but" to "and").	
Values: Keeping values in the forefront of your mind; putting your long-term mind in charge (rather than short-term mind).	

Worksheet 17-1 How Do You Compare to the NWCR Members?

Instructions: Take some time to reflect on whether you are engaging in key behaviors that are similar to those of NWCR members. Next to each behavior, indicate whether you have become similar to a successful weight loser.

Registry Members	You
Eat a low-calorie diet	☐ Currently achieving! ☐ Almost there. ☐ I'd like to work on this.
Have a high intake of a variety of fruits and vegetables	☐ Currently achieving! ☐ Almost there. ☐ I'd like to work on this.
Eat breakfast	☐ Currently achieving! ☐ Almost there. ☐ I'd like to work on this.
Eat five times a day	☐ Currently achieving! ☐ Almost there. ☐ I'd like to work on this.
Exercise for 1 hour per day	☐ Currently achieving! ☐ Almost there. ☐ I'd like to work on this.
Weigh self at least once per week	☐ Currently achieving! ☐ Almost there. ☐ I'd like to work on this.
Follow plan even on weekends and holidays	☐ Currently achieving! ☐ Almost there. ☐ I'd like to work on this.
Go to fast-food restaurants less than once per week	☐ Currently achieving! ☐ Almost there. ☐ I'd like to work on this.

Worksheet 17-2 Your Weight Maintenance Plan for Success

Instructions: Consider the strategies that successful weight maintainers in the NWCR report. Are there any that you are not doing currently but that might be helpful to consider for your own weight maintenance plan? Perhaps there are some behaviors that you did earlier in the program but have discontinued or ones that you'd thought about but never tried. **Select at least one additional weight maintenance strategy to incorporate into your maintenance plan.**

I already do the following to aid me in maintaining my weight loss:

1. _____

2. _____

3. _____

To help increase my success in weight maintenance, I plan to start:

1. _____

2. _____

3. _____

Set aside a few minutes to reflect on your accomplishments. What strategies are working for you to control your weight?

_____

_____

_____

What would it take for you to be eligible for the NWCR? What new strategies do you think are *most* important for you to focus on moving forward?

_____

_____

_____

Worksheet 17-3 Using Psychological Strategies to Maintain Weight Control Behaviors

We know that keeping up behaviors that have led to the success of NWCR members is difficult in the long term. Psychological skills can help motivate you to keep up with these behaviors. Name two or three NWCR behaviors you want to maintain and describe a psychological strategy that will help you with that behavior.

Here are some examples of skills we have discussed:

- **Willingness**: Engaging in a valued behavior despite internal discomfort, loss of pleasure
- **Defusion**: Getting distance from an internal experience in order to see it for what it really is (e.g., see a thought as just a thought)
- **Mindful decision-making**: Slowing down the decision-making process; making every decision an up or down vote on a value
- **Values**: Keeping values at the forefront of your mind

Behavior consistent with NWCR recommendations:	Psychological strategy I will use to help me maintain this behavior:
Example: I will walk 1 hour before breakfast every day	*Willingness: I will start my walk even if I'm tired or would rather do something else*

Worksheet 18-1 Overcoming Barriers to Physical Activity

Instructions: Over the next week, name or describe three barriers or challenges to physical activity you face, as well as a behavioral and/or willingness strategy you use to overcome it. If you don't experience any barriers over the next week, name a barrier and strategy you've used in the past. Choose from the following strategies:

Possible Behavioral Strategies:	Possible Willingness Strategies:
▪ Planning ▪ Break activity into 10-minute blocks ▪ Choose a different place or time to exercise ▪ Make myself accountable to someone/something ▪ Other strategies that have helped you become physically active	▪ Just do it! (no matter what your mind is telling you) ▪ Change "only if" to "even if" ▪ "Up" or "down" vote on a value ▪ "I'm having the thought/feeling that ..." ▪ Change "but" to "and"

Physical Activity Challenge/ Barrier	Behavioral and/or Willingness Strategy Used (name all that apply)	Outcome
Example: It's raining outside	Changed "only if to "even if" Changed the place of exercise	Used a DVD to get physical activity indoors

Committed Action = Maintaining behaviors that are consistent with one's values

Instructions: Reflect on the idea of committed action over the next few weeks. List five commitments (not including yours from group) that you want to aim for over the next two weeks. These commitments should be specific and easily measurable. After listing your commitments, think about any **potential challenges** you foresee in maintaining these. Once you have listed challenges, brainstorm strategies that you can use to address these potential challenges.

Commitment	Potential Challenges	Strategies to Enhance Commitment

Worksheet 20-1 Identifying Triggers of Overeating

Am I more likely to overeat when alone or with others? Are there certain people with whom I tend to overeat ("eating buddies")?

_____

_____

Do I overeat during certain times of the day or during certain activities (e.g., in the evening watching TV; at social events)?

_____

_____

Do I overeat in response to certain feelings or moods (e.g., depression, guilt, anxiety)?

_____

_____

Do I overeat in response to stressful events (either single events or the accumulation of daily hassles)?

_____

_____

Worksheet 20-2 Rate Your Emotional Eating

Emotional Eating Scale. We all respond to different emotions differently. Some types of feelings lead people to experience an urge to eat. Please indicate the extent to which the following feelings lead you to feel an urge to eat.

Total value: _____

	No Desire to Eat	A Small Desire to Eat	A Moderate Desire to Eat	A Strong Urge to Eat	An Overwhelming Urge to Eat
Resentful	☐	☐	☐	☐	☐
Discouraged	☐	☐	☐	☐	☐
Shaky	☐	☐	☐	☐	☐
Worn Out	☐	☐	☐	☐	☐
Inadequate	☐	☐	☐	☐	☐
Excited	☐	☐	☐	☐	☐
Rebellious	☐	☐	☐	☐	☐
Blue	☐	☐	☐	☐	☐
Jittery	☐	☐	☐	☐	☐
Sad	☐	☐	☐	☐	☐
Uneasy	☐	☐	☐	☐	☐
Irritated	☐	☐	☐	☐	☐
Jealous	☐	☐	☐	☐	☐
Worried	☐	☐	☐	☐	☐
Frustrated	☐	☐	☐	☐	☐
Lonely	☐	☐	☐	☐	☐
Furious	☐	☐	☐	☐	☐
On edge	☐	☐	☐	☐	☐
Confused	☐	☐	☐	☐	☐
Nervous	☐	☐	☐	☐	☐
Angry	☐	☐	☐	☐	☐
Guilty	☐	☐	☐	☐	☐
Bored	☐	☐	☐	☐	☐
Helpless	☐	☐	☐	☐	☐
Upset	☐	☐	☐	☐	☐
VALUE	*(1)*	*(2)*	*(3)*	*(4)*	*(5)*

Score	Emotional Eating Severity
0–30	Low
31–60	Medium
61–90	High
91–125	Very High

Source: Arnow, B., Kenardy, J., & Agras, W. S. (1995). The emotional eating scale: The development of a measure to assess coping with negative affect by eating. *International Journal of Eating Disorders, 18,* 79–90. Reprinted by permission of John Wiley & Sons Ltd.

Worksheet 20-3 Healthy Behaviors I Will Choose in Response to Difficult Emotions

Eating in response to difficult emotions is a habit that is reinforced by short-term success: the discomfort you experience lessens temporarily after eating. To enable change to take place, you can develop a new response to difficult emotions that is more consistent with your values. Choose a new set of (more adaptive and/or more values-consistent) behaviors that you will purposely choose in response to emotions that trigger eating. In the space below, name behaviors that you can choose in the face of difficult feelings that will help you feel balanced, sooth you, promote health, and solve a difficult problem.

Behaviors That Help Me Feel Balanced

    1. _____

    2. _____

Behaviors That Soothe Me

    1. _____

    2. _____

Behaviors That Promote Health

    1. _____

    2. _____

Behaviors That Solve a Problem

    1. _____

    2. _____

Name a situation when you were aware of an emotion:	What was your response to your emotion?	What are two healthy responses to that emotion?
		1. 2.
		1. 2.
		1. 2.
		1. 2.
		1. 2.

Worksheet 21-1 High-Risk Situations

Emotional High-Risk Situations

1. You earned a promotion and want to treat yourself to a meal and a cocktail at a nice restaurant.

2. You are on a family trip, feeling relaxed and enjoying the time away.

3. You feel overwhelmed by stressors outside of your control.

4. You've been feeling down or lonely.

5. You feel irritable, annoyed, or upset.

6. _____

7. _____

8. _____

9. _____

High-Risk Breaks in Routine

1. You are on vacation and staying with a friend or in a hotel.

2. You're on a business trip and dining out often.

3. There isn't anything scheduled for the weekend, and you don't have any activities to keep you busy.

4. You have an injury or feel under the weather and can't do your usual routine.

5. Things are hectic at work or at home.

6. You are visiting a loved one in the hospital often.

7. _____

8. _____

9. _____

Social High-Risk Situations

1. There is a birthday party in your office and your coworkers are all having cake.

2. You go to a friend's house for a potluck dinner and most of the options are high-calorie dishes.

3. Your supervisor invites you out to lunch.

4. You have an argument with someone you respect.

5. There is tension in your family.

6. Your family members are disappointed about the low-calorie meal you made and plead for take-out instead.

7. _____

8. _____

9. _____

Other High-Risk Situations

High-Risk Negative Physical States	High-Risk Urges and Temptations
1. You feel fatigued or worn out.	1. You find tasty, high-calorie treats in your pantry that you didn't know were there.
2. You are awake in the middle of the night.	2. You have a craving for a certain food.
3. You are sick or coming down with a cold.	3. A loved one gives you candy as a gift.
4. _____	4. _____
5. _____	5. _____

Worksheet 21-2 My Behavioral Action Plan for High-Risk Situations

- I am at high risk for stopping my healthy eating when:

_____

_____

✓ My plan to handle this situation so that I don't slip or lapse is:

_____

_____

_____

- I am at high risk for decreasing my physical activity when:

_____

_____

✓ My plan to handle this situation so that I don't slip or lapse is:

_____

_____

_____

- I am at high risk for missing a session or not recording on my Keeping Track Form when:

_____

_____

✓ My plan to handle this situation so that I don't slip or lapse is:

_____

_____

Worksheet 21-3 My Psychological Action Plan for High-Risk Situations

What psychological factors are related to my lapses?

(Circle any that apply or add your own)

- Mindless eating and/or physical activity decisions

- Lowered motivation

- Eroded commitment

- Lack of willingness to experience loss of pleasure or cravings for high-calorie food

- Lack of willingness to engage in physical activity rather than staying at rest

- Difficulty defusing from strong emotions such as boredom, guilt, sadness

- Difficulty defusing from thoughts that undermine unhealthy decisions (e.g., "one cookie won't hurt")

- _____

- _____

What can I do to handle these lapses?

(Circle any that apply or add your own)

- Redouble efforts to increase mindful, deliberate choices

- Commit to healthy behavioral choices even if doing so creates or leaves in place unpleasant thoughts or feelings

- Increase willingness to experience difficult thoughts, feelings, and urges

- See thoughts for what they are (just thoughts) and not for what they say they are

- _____

- _____

- _____

- _____

Worksheet 21-4 My Plan for Reversing a Small Weight Gain

My Red Zone weight: _____ lbs.

My Goal Weight: _____ lbs.

Behaviors and strategies that will help me reverse my weight gain:

1. _____

_____

_____

2. _____

_____

_____

3. _____

_____

_____

4. _____

_____

_____

5. _____

_____

_____

Worksheet 22-1 Recommitment!

Instructions: Please identify times when you slipped (e.g., gave up on your commitment) or times when there was a potential to slip. Record the challenges that you faced to keep your commitment. If you slipped, what strategy could you use to recommit? If you succeeded in keeping your commitment, how were you able to do so?

Situation	What made it difficult to stick to your commitment?	How did you/can you recommit?

Worksheet 23-1 Visual Reminders to Stay Motivated

We have talked about how it is difficult to maintain motivation in the weight maintenance phase. Having specific ways to stay motivated is helpful. One thing we have discussed is placing visual reminders (post-it notes, pictures, symbolic jewelry, etc.) in your day-to-day environment (car, work, home, bathroom, etc.) to help remind you of the things that you care about most. What visual reminders will enable you to stay *aware of* and *connected to* your values?

Instructions: Please choose five very specific examples of visual reminders that you can place in your environment over the next month and spend the next month saturating your environment with these reminders.

1. _____

2. _____

3. _____

4. _____

5. _____

Worksheet 23-2 Are You Voting for What You Value?

Instructions: Be mindful of what you value and what values you are voting for with each behavior you engage in. At the end of each week, write down one value and one behavior you engaged in that was a vote for that value. Pick behaviors that were hard for you to do, because those are some of your most important votes.

	Value	Behavior
Example	Being physically active	Riding my bike home from work on Tuesday even though I felt tired and it would have been easier to take the bus
Week 1		
Week 2		
Week 3		
Week 4		

Instructions: There are several key behaviors that will maximize your weight control success in the future. For each key behavior, answer the questions and write down the key behavioral and psychological strategies you will need to implement in order to maintain this behavior in the long term.

Key Behavior 1: Self-monitor your weight. **Weigh yourself at least weekly. Daily weighing may be most helpful.**	
How important is this behavior as part of your long-term weight control plan? *(Circle one)*	*Not at all important* *Somewhat important* *Very important* *Critically important*
What is your personal goal for this behavior?	I will weigh myself _____ times per _____.
What could make it hard to meet this goal over the next six months?	1. 2.
What is one key behavioral and psychological strategy you will use to maintain this behavior long-term?	1. 2.

Key Behavior 2: Limit calorie intake.
To maintain weight loss, calorie intake must stay below what it was at previous higher weights.

How important is this behavior as part of your long-term weight control plan? *(Circle one)*	*Not at all important* *Somewhat important* *Very important* *Critically important*
What is your personal goal for this behavior?	I will eat _____ calories per day.
What could make it hard to meet this goal over the next six months?	1. 2.
What is one key behavioral and psychological strategy you will use to maintain this behavior long term?	1. 2.

Key Behavior 3: Engage in high levels of physical activity.
Completing 250 minutes of activity per week will help prevent weight regain.

How important is this behavior as part of your long-term weight control plan? *(Circle one)*	*Not at all important* *Somewhat important* *Very important* *Critically important*
What is your personal goal for this behavior?	I will exercise _____ minutes per day, _____ days per week.
What could make it hard to meet this goal over the next six months?	1. 2.
What is one key behavioral and psychological strategy you will use to maintain this behavior long-term?	1. 2.

Worksheet 25-1 Celebrating Accomplishments

Instructions: Take some time to reflect on what you have accomplished and learned during this program by answering the questions below.

Strategies you've used to be more active:

_____

_____

_____

The biggest challenge you have overcome to make changes in your physical activity:

_____

_____

_____

The physical activity change that you are proudest of:

_____

_____

_____

Strategies you've used to eat fewer calories:

_____

_____

_____

The biggest challenge you have overcome to make changes in your diet:

_____

_____

_____

The change in your diet that you are proudest of:

_____

_____

_____

How do you plan to stay on track in the absence of these sessions? How will you receive the support you need?

_____

_____

_____

Source: Look AHEAD Research Group. (2001). "Session 44: Congratulations—You've completed one year of the Look AHEAD lifestyle program!" In *Action for health in diabetes: Look AHEAD clinical trial lifestyle intervention— Year 1 manual*. Retrieved from https://www.lookaheadtrial.org/public/dspMaterials.cfm. Adapted with permission from Look AHEAD.